PARIS ALONG THE SEINE

BETWEEN PONT D'AUSTERLITZ AND PONT DE GRENELLE

This simplified map of Paris along the Seine, between the Pont d'Austerlitz and the Pont de Grenelle, serves to identify the names of the bridges numbered on the map, as well as some of the principal buildings, monuments, and boulevards. The Seine is purposely shown triple its actual width in order to: (1) provide space for numerals identifying each bridge, even when densely huddled as from 3 to 5, and (2) show at the river's banks whether there is both an upper *and* lower quai ("porte"), by means of a double line (as exists all along the Right Bank), or if there is only an upper quai at street level, shown by a single line (as on the Ile de la Cité from 4 to 5, and from 12 to 15).

Because the width of the Seine is emphasized, the map is slightly distorted at the lower left (southwest). Otherwise, it is reasonably accurate.

Gerald K. Geerlings

PARIS ALONG THE SEINE • GERALD K. GEERLINGS

N E S W

1 2 3 4 5 6 7 8

A

1-Theatre du Châtelet / 2-Theatre de Sarah Bernhardt / 3-Hotel de Ville / 4-St. Gervais / 5-Statue of Henri IV in Square du Vert Gallant / 6-Spire of Ste. Chapell

The Pont-Neuf as viewed from the Pont des Arts

Left Bank

-Spire of Notre Dame / A - Quai du Louvre / B - Quai de Conti

Gerald K. Geerlings

PARIS ALONG THE SEINE • GERALD K. GEERLINGS

Foreword by
Marie-Madeleine Fourcade

Notes by
Jean-Marie Besset

French Institute/Alliance Française

Cedar Rapids Museum of Art

Translation French Institute / Alliance Francaise
Published with a grant from
The Florence J. Gould Foundation, New York.
Drawings from the collection of the Association
Amicale Alliance, Paris.
Endpapers: Map of Paris along the Seine,
    Gerald K. Geerlings, 1976.
Drawings © 1987 Gerald K. Geerlings
Text © 1987 French Institute / Alliance Francaise
    and Cedar Rapids Museum of Art
Distributed by: Cedar Rapids Museum of Art,
    428 Third Ave. S.E.
    Cedar Rapids, Iowa 52401
    Telephone: (319) 366-7503

    French Institute / Alliance Francaise,
    22 East 60th Street,
    New York, New York 10022
    Telephone: (212) 355-6100.

Library of Congress Cataloging in Publication
Data.

Geerlings, Gerald K. (Gerald Kenneth), 1897-
    Paris along the Seine / Gerald Geerlings;
    foreword by Marie-Madeleine Fourcade.
    ISBN 0-942982-03-7
    1. Geerlings, Gerald K. (Gerald Kenneth),
    1897-   . 2. Drawing, American. 3. Draw-
    ing, Modern — 20th century — United States.
    4. Paris (France) in art. 5. Seine River
    (France) in art.
    I. Title.
    NC139.G233A4   1987
    741.973—dc19   87-34210

Printed in the United States of America.

Acknowledgements

Jean Vallier
Joseph S. Czestochowski

Gerald K. Geerlings is a rare individual who has achieved distinguished results in a variety of career pursuits. He is a decorated soldier, the author of several standard texts on architectural history and design, an architect of considerable merit, a respected graphic and industrial designer, and an artist of substantial technical and aesthetic virtuosity. In short, he is a humanist who has created eloquent visual statements that are fresh, sensitive, pragmatic, and at times, romantic.

Geerlings' works are treasured by institutions and collectors, both in the United States and abroad. He is not a prolific artist, but his work is exceptional. Since the 1920s, Geerlings' predominant interest has been the cityscape. His primary challenge has been to extract the essence of a subject. In achieving this goal, he has demonstrated exquisite draftsmanship and perceptive composition. These attributes pervade the drawings that are the subject of this volume.

Preoccupied throughout his life by urban planning, Geerlings found in Paris a subject well-suited to his strengths. The Paris drawings occupied Geerlings for much of his life and in many ways grew from his partnership with his wife of sixty-two years. Betty Geerlings was a warm individual whose infectious enthusiasm won out over painful distractions. The Geerlings' shared sense of adventure and enjoyment is readily evident in these sensitive and informative works. They are in many respects an enduring testimony to a marriage marked by support, balance, and encouragement.

Thanks are also due to Jacqueline Chambord of the French Institute/Alliance Française, John R. Young of The Florence J. Gould Foundation, Inc., and his wife, Mary. Each individual shared a decisive role in the publication of this volume. Finally, we are grateful to Gerald K. Geerlings for allowing others to share his vision of Paris along the Seine.

Foreword

Marie-Madeleine Fourcade

"I like to look out of my window at the Seine (Quai Malaquais) and its quais on those soft gray mornings which give such an infinite tenderness of tint to everything. I have seen the azure sky which flings so luminous and calm over the Bay of Naples. But our Parisian sky is more animated, more tender, more spiritual. It smiles, threatens, caresses, takes an aspect of melancholy or a look of merriment like a human gaze."

— Anatole France, *Crime of Sylvester Bonnard.*

Albufeira, Algarve 1972
(Pentel-black)

Gerald K. Geerlings spent four years of his life, from 1971 to 1975, drawing *Paris along the Seine*. He calls the river "the most beautiful avenue of the world," and conceived of the project not only to document bridges, monuments, and nearby gardens of Paris, but also to create a volume dedicated to the French Resistance.

Born April 18, 1897 in Milwaukee, Wisconsin, Gerald K. Geerlings served in the First World War. Joining at the age of 19, he was in the 120th Field Artillery, 32nd Division (National Guards of Wisconsin and Michigan). Appointed Second Lieutenant, he did his training in Saumur and remained 18 months in Paris with the expeditionary forces.

Back in the army in 1942 as Captain in the Army Air Corps, Geerlings took part in some of the most notable European battles of the Second World War, such as the Sicilian and the Italian campaigns, the battle of

Ploesti, ending with the Japanese campaign as intelligence officer to headquarters of the 8th Air Force Bomber Command.

While serving on board heavy bombers during daylight missions, he became convinced that the execution of such endeavors depended entirely on the information provided by the Resistance at the cost of inestimable sacrifices. He was perfectly aware, too, of the debt all the aviators coming down in France owed to the Resistance networks that ensured their safety and led them through the Pyrenees. Geerlings felt profoundly how little acknowledgement these countless sacrifices and extraordinary exploits had received.

For these reasons, he wished to associate, in an inalienable way for future generations, the Seine's course, lined with its extraordinary environment of monumental architecture and centenary trees, to the heroic French Resistance.

The artist's abiding desire to honor the spirit of the Resistance Forces is consistent with his own ancestry, going back five generations through his grandfather to Michel Le Tellier, Chancellor of France, Guardian of the Seal, and Counsellor of Sun King Louis XIV. Thus, Gerald Geerlings is a true comrade in arms.

That his drawings, executed with passion, serve to keep alive the spirit of the French Resistance and heal the subsisting wounds of the aftermath is his fondest wish.

Marie-Madeleine Fourcade was Chief of the Network Alliance combat unit during 1940-45 and has been President of the Comité d'Action de la Résistance française since 1963.

Introduction

Gerald K. Geerlings

No other city has a site that compares with the seven-mile esplanade of Paris which extends from the Pont d'Austerlitz upstream, down to, and including the Pont de Grenelle, where the original and much smaller Statue of Liberty is located. Upstream and downstream from these two bridges, the dismaying evidence of commercialism is not a wit less obnoxious than that which disfigures waterfront property in all other cities. But these seven miles—what a treasury of ideas for the urban planner, the transportation expert, the art lover, and the everyday tourist! The esplanade has three levels: (1) the river for barge traffic from ports as distant as Holland and Belgium, (2) the lower level quais or "portes," consisting of walkways and "autoroutes" about five feet above the water level, and (3) the street level for vehicular traffic and walkways, which often include vest pocket parks or widen out in continuous parkways complete with sandboxes and benches.

The commercial traffic consists of barges as long as a Manhattan city block which busily play up and down during daylight hours. Yet their variety and animation add rather than detract from the overall effect of civic beauty. I marvel at the grace of oncoming barges, perhaps as many as three in tandem, each loaded to the gunwales, aligned one ahead of the other, being pushed by what my wife and I long ago dubbed a "pusher-tug." The barges are so gracefully maneuvered that when a change of direction is necessary to thread them through a relatively narrow arch, as at the Pont des Arts, this elongated assemblage, of maybe 500 feet or more, accurately clears the hazards of the bridge piers.

Well-travelled critics rank Paris along the Seine among the greatest works of art in Europe. The seven miles incorporate the disciplines of architecture, landscape architecture, sculpture, and engineering. Start a discussion by asking if there is any other city in Europe where all of the former are combined to create an equally satisfying aesthetic result. Evaluate the segments of beautiful waterfronts or esplanades of any other city and record their extent. Some may deserve high marks for a few hundred yards. But try to find any which total one mile in length, let alone *seven*. Loyalists for nominating this Paris esplanade as the foremost work of art in Europe have in their favor the fact that it can be viewed at any hour of the day, any day of the year, in any kind of weather. In contrast, most treasures in sculpture, painting, tapestry, or ceramics can be viewed for a fee in museums only on certain days of the week and only during specified hours.

Most works of art can be attributed to a single person. Not so the Incredible Seven Miles. For some 800 years the royal or civic temptation to derive fabulous income from selling or leasing sites along this stretch has been resisted. What a miracle! Through the centuries reigning monarchs have levied heavy taxes on their groaning subjects to satisfy their extravagant needs. Yet never on this esplanade has there been the financial exploitation which exists along the Seine on the outskirts of Paris.

My wife and I began our European travels a week after we were married, in September of 1924. Over the 62 years of our married life we explored cities extending from the Atlantic Ocean on the west to Istanbul on the east, from North Africa on the south to almost the Arctic Circle on the north. I took numerous photographs and made a considerable quantity of drawings. In 1968 I decided to let my New York State architect's license lapse and devote full time to my first love doing cityscapes in various media. By then I had subconsciously made the decision to record (and hopefully do justice) to the unrivaled urban solution of Paris along the Seine.

This was not without qualms. I was well aware that the Musée Carnavalet of Paris had vast collections of paintings of Paris, many on display, still more in storage. I was well-acquainted with the magnificent etchings by Charles Meryon, as well as Impressionist paintings of scenes along the Seine. Dutifully and reverently my wife and I examined at the Carnavalet Museum what paintings there are of the Seine esplanade, but we were soon forced to conclude that there is no continuity of records along the Seine at any single period of time. Even if what exists were to be adroitly assembled for an exhibition, the most intelligent observer would be unable to form a clear idea of what the Seine esplanade as a whole actually was or is. So, since I yearned to spend a planned slice of time drawing in Paris, why not try to record "Paris along the Seine"?

I offer this book: (1) to those who know Paris, who rejoice in their memories along the Seine and the continued preservation of the longest, most beautiful "street" in Europe, (2) to those who have never been to Paris, but, hoping to go sometime, will find the book worth buying as a succinct guide to the main artery of Paris, (3) to those who wish to give a noncontroversial book to someone who has been or will be going to France, (4) to those who are attracted to the illustrations per se, and to the brief historical summary about each subject, and (5) to those who are involved or interested in urban planning, and who lament that the cores of practically all cities are dying. We can rejoice together that the contrary is true of Paris.

About The Bridges

Jean-Marie Besset
(Translation: Hal J. Witt)

The Pont-Neuf

The most famous of the Paris bridges is also the one that has kept its most original appearance. Apart from a few details, it remains as it appeared on June 20, 1603 to King Henri IV, who was the first to cross it.

We owe the splendid restoration to the Second Empire. Lacking proper maintenance after its construction, the bridge was a ruin in 1848. A general repair rebuilt entirely its twelve arcades, its stone facade, the parapet and corniche, while eliminating the shops which had been added in 1775 in the half-moons above the piers. The Pont-Neuf connects the Rue Dauphine (Left Bank) and the Rue de la Monnaie (Right Bank) while touching down midway on the tip of the Ile de la Cité.

In the middle of the 16th century, the development of the University of Paris, the increase of traffic, and the fragility of the Change and Notre-Dame bridges (overloaded by the houses they bore) made a new bridge necessary. Because this spot between the Louvre and the Hôtel de Nesles was also a deadly trap resulting from the complicity of boat-crossers and robbers, a bridge was considered there as a public safety measure as early as 1556.

On May 31, 1578, Henri III arrived on a magnificent boat with the queen mother Catherine de Médicis to lay the first stone. In spite of the efforts of Androuet du Cerceau, the King's young architect, the work was not finished before the Civil War. The King, however, showed a great interest in the construction and was anxious to see the bridge completed. One winter, he had a wooden footpath suspended from the unfinished piers between the two banks and crossed with his Court to go to a feast given in the Grands-Augustins in honor of the new Order of the Holy Ghost. That was the only time Henri III was able to cross "his" bridge, which was finally completed after the war, under Henri IV.

Therefore, it is a statue of the latter which was erected in 1614 on the Pont-Neuf by order of his son, King Louis XIII. The present statue is a Second Empire copy of the original, destroyed during the Revolution when a "bleu blanc rouge" flag was put in his place.

The Pont-Neuf was the first bridge of Paris to have been built without houses above. It would soon become the center of Parisian Life, a proverb claimed that, at any hour of the day, you could see a white horse, a courtesan, and a monk there.

The Pont Saint-Michel

Like the Change Bridge whose traverse across the Seine it continues from the Boulevard du Palais to the Place Saint-Michel

(Left Bank), the present Saint-Michel Bridge can be credited to the Second Empire.

Also decorated with "N"s and laurels, these three arches made of stone assembled with cement were the work of the engineer Vaudrey.

Until the end of the 14th century, the "Petit Pont" was the only link between the Ile de la Cité and the Left Bank. In 1378, it was decided to build the first Saint-Michel Bridge. It was finished under Charles VI in 1387 and named after a chapel on a little square between the Sainte-Chapelle and the Rue Saint-Michel where King Philippe Auguste was baptized.

The Petit Pont

The Petit Pont, between the quais of Montebello (Left Bank) and the Marché-Neuf (on the Ile de la Cité) remains the shortest bridge in Paris at 120 feet. Consisting of one arch of stone and cement, it replaced for navigational purposes — an elegant work in three arches from the beginning of the 18th century.

A very colorful French expression has its origin in this bridge: "payer en monnaie de singe" (to pay with monkey-money: not to pay at all) refers to an unusual exception to the toll which was fixed in 1206:

"The merchant who brings a monkey to sell in Paris will pay 4 deniers, but if the monkey belongs to a man making the animal play and dance, the toll will be the monkey and everything else he has brought with him on this trip."

The Pont-au-Double

At the beginning of the 17th century, the construction of new hospitals in Paris could not alleviate the crowding of the Hôtel-Dieu, Paris' oldest hospital. It was therefore decided in 1626 to build a bridge to support additional buildings with rooms for the sick. The riverside residents asked for a public passage (one third of the width of the path) to enable crossing from the square of Notre-Dame to the Left Bank. Louis XIII fixed the toll for the horsemen at twice that of the pedestrians; hence the "Double" Bridge.

Increasing traffic on the bridge, extensive navigation underneath, and the campaign for the destruction of the houses on the Paris bridges caused the bridge to be destroyed and rebuilt several times. The present cast-iron arch was built in 1882. It is difficult to imagine in its place the "Pont-aux-ânes" (Donkeys' Bridge) of the Middle Ages. There the livestock used to cross to graze in the meadows now occupied by the Entrepôt and the Jardin des Plantes.

The Pont de l'Archevêché

This bridge links the Left Bank and the Quai de l'Archevêché, at the level of the Square Jean XXIII. Here, at the eastern end of the Ile de la Cité, Charlotte of Savoy, second spouse of King Louis XI, landed to enter Paris in 1407.

The bridge was started under Charles X in April 1828 and opened to traffic the following November, a very fast job indeed for this impressive work of masonry with three arches.

The former Episcopal Palace, on the side of Notre-Dame, which gave the bridge its name, was ransacked and burnt on February 15, 1831 by rioters dressed in Carnival costumes. They were enraged by word that the Legitimists had celebrated a mass commemorating the anniversary of the murder of the Duke of Berry.

The Pont de la Tournelle

The bridge owes its name to a square tower built under Philippe Auguste to protect, along with the Lauriot Tower on the Ile Saint-Louis and the Billy Tower on the Right Bank, the entrance to Paris on the Seine. Later, the Tournelle Tower became a prison and remained so until 1790.

As early as the 14th century, there is mention of a wooden bridge there, called "the log bridge of the Ile Notre-Dame," which linked the island to the Left Bank. Destroyed and rebuilt many times, always in wood, it was expanded in 1620 by Christophe Marie, who intended to coordinate with the real estate development he was carrying out on the island.

Because of a series of terrible floods, a stone bridge with six arches finally replaced the wooden one in the middle of the 17th century.

The present bridge gives a poor idea of the character of the old one, built under the Sun King. Made of concrete and covered with carved stones, the new bridge is composed of one large central arch and two smaller lateral ones. Its profile is spoiled by what appears as a sort of white rocket actually a diminutive Sainte Geneviève on a sleek pedestal by the sculptor Landowski.

The Pont Sully

This bridge actually consists of two metallic bridges built between 1874 and 1876 to link the Boulevard Saint-Germain (Left Bank) and the Boulevard Henri IV (Right Bank). It meets on the Ile Saint-Louis where, apart from the old Bertillon storefront, one currently finds the modern hideaways of writers and the pieds-a-terre of Americans.

Until 1933 the Sully "bridges" coexisted with an ancient footbridge of wooden scaf-

PARIS ALONG THE SEINE

BETWEEN PONT D'AUSTERLITZ AND PONT DE GRENELLE

This simplified map of Paris along the Seine, between the Pont d'Austerlitz and the Pont de Grenelle, serves to identify the names of the bridges numbered on the map, as well as some of the principal buildings, monuments, and boulevards. The Seine is purposely shown triple its actual width in order to: (1) provide space for numerals identifying each bridge, even when densely huddled as from 3 to 5, and (2) show at the river's banks whether there is both an upper *and* lower quai ("porte"), by means of a double line (as exists all along the Right Bank), or if there is only an upper quai at street level, shown by a single line (as on the Ile de la Cité from 4 to 5, and from 12 to 15).

Because the width of the Seine is emphasized, the map is slightly distorted at the lower left (southwest). Otherwise, it is reasonably accurate.

Gerald K. Geerlings

folding that ran between the upriver end of the island and the Quai Henri IV. The scaffolding sheltered the boats parked in the port of the Célestins-Saint-Paul, on the little arm of the Seine, from drifting blocks of ice at the end of the winter. This was rather fragile protection, since the scaffolding, when it was not on fire, was often itself destroyed by the ice blocks.

When the southern part of the bridge was built, the tip of the medieval city of King Philippe Auguste was excavated, together with the base of the historic Tournelle Tower.

The Pont d'Austerlitz

Designed by the engineer Becquey-Beaupré, this bridge was inaugurated to celebrate Napoleon's victory at Austerlitz on December 2, 1805. It linked the Place Mazas and the Place Valhubert, named after two officers who fell on the Austerlitz battlefield. Newspapers of the time note "the magnificence of the site in which the bridge is thrown." This contrasts regrettably with the ugliness of the buildings that now form a backdrop to the bridge along the Quai de la Rapée.

The Second empire, willing to use its gold to celebrate the glories of the First, replaced the iron bridge with a stone bridge in 1855. The iron arches had begun to crack under the increasing traffic between the Orleans and Lyons train stations. A further enlargement occurred in 1885, again in response to increased traffic.

The Pont Marie

At the end of the 13th century, the Ile Saint-Louis (formerly Ile Notre-Dame) was one of the sacred places from which the Crusades were launched.

It long remained without any links to the "civilized" banks of the Seine or the Ile-de-la-Cité. Bridges would have been useless anyway, for the island was uninhabited and divided by a large ditch that made the site unsuitable for construction.

On April 19, 1614 an act of King Louis XIII authorized the developer Christophe Marie to fill the ditch and to build at his own expense a stone bridge to link the quartier Saint-Paul on the Right Bank with the Island's Tournelle area. In exchange for his bridge, Christophe Marie obtained "a deed in perpetuity to the estate and property which His Majesty gives to him of the two islands of Our Lady." It seems that Mr. Marie was a pioneer in real estate speculation. The bridge was completed in 1635.

Marie had also obtained the privilege of "building on the bridge houses of the same size and height, provided that they would leave sufficient space for a street." The terrible flood which submerged half of the city in 1658 swept half of the bridge away. The weight of the houses was deemed unsafe and the unfortunate inhabitants of the homes spared by the flood were threatened with eviction in 1666.

A subsequent flood in 1740 was even worse: "The river has overflowed and, on all sides, everyone is seeking refuge on the upper floors. All the inhabitants of the Ile Notre-Dame are stranded," a witness reported. The city magistrates finally took exceptional measures with the edict of 1741, prescribing the destruction of all houses on the Paris bridges.

The Pont Louis-Philippe

In July 1834 King Louis Philippe inaugurated a bridge linking the Quai de la Grève (Right Bank) to the Ile de la Cité. It was suspended from a triumphal arch erected on the western end of the Ile Saint-Louis, which made the neighbouring Cité footbridge (presently Saint-Louis Bridge) superfluous.

The bridge was renamed "of the Reformation" in the euphoria of the 1848 Revolution, but the new name proved even more ephemeral than the Second Republic. Soon after, the bridge itself was destroyed by a fire which broke its chains and caused the entire pathway to fall into the Seine.

Rebuilt with stone in a more traditional configuration in 1860, it regained, under the emperor, the name of the King of the French.

The Pont Saint-Louis

Christophe Marie, the developer of the Ile Saint-Louis, who had linked his island to the Right Bank (Marie Bridge) and Left (La Tournelle Bridge), was allowed to build a wooden bridge so that the island residents could go to mass by foot without having to go the long way around by the banks.

The Council of Notre-Dame opposed the

project for some time. Finally, in exchange for its permission to build the bridge, the Council gained the free use of 30 feet on the Quai of the neighbouring Saint-Landry Port along with a promise that neither the priests nor their servants would pay the toll instituted by Christophe Marie.

On June 5, 1634 three processions tried to cross all at once to go to Notre-Dame and the bridge partially collapsed. Two years later, in anticipation of the Jubilee celebrations, two wooden fences were installed at each entrance to the bridge.

In 1710, a new wooden bridge was built there, called "red bridge" because of the minium paint that was used to protect the wood from humidity. At the time, a witness laughed at the "weird and ridiculous construction which shames Paris where everything should look strong and magnificent." The judgement of this man of the Enlightenment could as easily apply to the crude

present bridge which in 1970 replaced a temporary footpath that had been installed in 1941. The latter replaced a bridge of nine cast iron arches built under Napoleon III which was destroyed by an 800 ton barge that crashed into it in December 1939.

The Pont d'Arcole

A modest bridge was erected on this site in 1828. It was named "Pont de Grève" after the name of the quai (Right Bank) bordering the Hôtel de Ville (Town Hall). On July 28, 1830, during the attempt to revive the Republic, the people rushed on the Pont de Grève against the troops defending the Hôtel de Ville. A young man carrying the flag took the head of a Republican group and ran forth on the bridge. Caught in the crossfire of the gendarmes, he fell, shouting something with the word "Arcole" in it. Was it his name? Was he invoking the Italian victory of Napoleon? The bridge was baptized Arcole in memory of this intrepid citizen.

The Pont Notre-Dame

The present bridge was built in 1853, at the time when the Rue de Rivoli reached and crossed the Rue Saint-Martin. Of the five vaults of the 1853 bridge, the three central ones were replaced in 1912 by a unique metallic arch which is less obtrusive for navigation.

As early as Roman times, there was at this crucial spot a wooden footbridge called "Grand Pont." Lutetia (the present Ile de la Cité) was indeed connected to the banks of the Seine by two bridges. One, called "Grand Pont" spanning the "big arm" of the river (Right Bank), the other called "Petit Pont" (Left Bank). In the Middle Ages, the two bridges formed a perfect North-South axis from the Porte Saint-Martin to the Porte Saint-Jacques.

In 1406, the bridge of the Mibray Plank successor of the Roman "Grand Pont" was destroyed by the flood. On May 31, 1413, the King dedicated the new wooden bridge, calling it the "Pont Notre-Dame" (Our Lady Bridge).

A century later, the bridge was rebuilt in stone and opened up with great fanfare on July 10, 1507. The bridge boasted sixty-eight identical beautiful houses (thirty-four on each side) all marked with gilded letters on a red background—apparently the first attempt to number the streets in France.

Thomas Coryate, a British visitor at the time, described this street on the Notre-Dame Bridge as the most beautiful of Paris.

The Pont-au-Change

For a long time, this bridge linked two prisons: the Conciergerie and the Châtelet. The former has become a museum and the latter a theatre.

The present bridge was rebuilt by

Haussmann in 1859-60 in order to be aligned with the new Boulevard du Palais (on the Ile de la Cité), which was designed at the same time, and the reorganized Place du Châtelet (Right Bank).

The three arches—built with stones salvaged from the bridge's predecessor—were erected in the middle of the 17th century by Jacques Androuet du Cerceau. The simple and majestic line of the bridge is enhanced above each pier by an initial in a crown of laurels: a bas-relief homage to the capital "N" by "the other" Napoleon.

In the 13th and 14th centuries, the houses on the bridge were inhabited by jewellers and currency-changers, hence its name.

Beginning in the 17th century, on Tuesdays and on Saturday mornings, the tree and flower market took place there and on Sundays, the pet and poultry market (now at the Quai de la Mégisserie on the Right Bank).

The Pont des Arts

The Bridge of the Arts has just been rebuilt. It was reopened to pedestrians in 1985, a few months too late for curious strollers to contemplate its neighbor, the Pont-Neuf, the talk of the town in its giant wrapping by the artist Christo.

Built between 1802 and 1804, the "Pont des Arts" was originally made of nine cast-iron arches (reduced to eight in 1852) laid on masonry piers. Until its destruction in 1981, the footpath remained the oldest example of metallic architecture in Paris.

It is unknown whether this footpath was baptized "des Arts" because it found itself in front of one of the Louvre gates or because it led (on the Left Bank) to the Collège des Quatre-Nations where Napoleon wanted to establish the Ecole des Beaux-Arts.

The magnificent restoration of the square courtyard of the Louvre, the crowds it draws, and the perspective it offers toward the Académie Française give the rebuilt Pont des Arts a new life.

The Pont du Carrousel

The present version of the Carrousel Bridge dates to 1939. Linking the Quai Voltaire (near the Rue des Saints-Pères) to the central part of the Louvre (where the triumphal arch of the same name is situated), the bridge is made of concrete with stones.

It replaced the original bridge (1834) designed by the engineer Polonceau, who invented a new process which enabled the construction of three cast-iron arches, each spanning 48 meters. Of this former bridge, all that remain are four statues by Petitôt, representing Abundancy and Industry, the Seine and the City of Paris (1846).

The bridge commemorates the feast of 1662 where, on a vast space in front of the Louvre, Louis XIV offered Mlle de la Vallière a magnificent live carrousel: bleachers for 15,000 spectators surrounded a ring with horsemen dressed as Romans, Persians, Indians, Turks, and "Americans."

The Pont-Royal

Built during 1685-89 and restored in 1839, the Royal Bridge is, together with the Pont-Neuf and the Marie bridges one of the three oldest in Paris. Its status as an "histori-cal monument" has sheltered it from destruction, suggested many times because the bridge does not coincide with any particular axis, leading as it does on the Right Bank to the Pavillon de Flore (Louvre) and on the Left Bank to a row of townhouses between the Rues du Bac and de Beaune. It is linked to the quais with cutaway panels, which ease the flow of traffic onto the bridge.

A gift from Louis XIV to Paris (hence its name) and the work of the famous architect Mansart, the Bridge Royal had replaced a wooden bridge which had been destroyed several times and had borne several names. Its last appellation of "Red Bridge" (it was covered with minium paint) was made famous during the flood of 1684 by a bon mot of Mme de Sévigné: "The Red Bridge departed for Saint-Cloud."

In the 18th century, the Royal Bridge was the platform from which one watched the great nautical festivals which took place on the Seine until construction of the Pont-Neuf.

The Pont Solferino

In front of the Tuileries gardens (Right Bank) the bridge Solferino was inaugurated on August 14, 1859, and baptized after the victory of Solferino, all—including the defeat of the Austrians—by Napoleon III. This metallic bridge of three arches required 1200 tons of cast-iron.

Demolished in 1959, it had yet to be replaced, except by a temporary footbridge.

The Pont de la Concorde

A highly symbolic bridge that links the Ancien Regime (the Place de la Concorde was called Place Louis XV) with the new one (National Assembly), its construction went on in the middle of the Revolution.

At the end of the 18th century, the

Faubourgs Saint-Germain (Left Bank) and Saint-Honoré (Right Bank) were first being developed. It soon became urgent to erect a bridge between the Place Louis XV and the birth of the boulevard Saint-Germain. An edict of Louis XVI ordered its construction. The work was assigned to engineer Perronet (1708-94), founder of the National School of Ponts et Chaussées (Bridges and Roads), whose innovations reduced the thickness of the piers and provided extra-low vaults.

The work was spread out over three years, from 1788 to 1791. The first stone laid (August 11, 1788) was obviously different from the others, which mostly came from the destroyed Bastille, "so that the people can perpetually crush under their feet the ancient fortress."

The width of the bridge was doubled in 1930-32, a well-planned renovation that happily kept the profile of the Perronet bridge.

The Pont Alexandre III

Along the axis that leads from the dome of the Invalides to the Champs-Elysées is the most beautiful of Paris bridges. It forms one of the three elements of a monumental perspective linking the Invalides esplanade and the Grand and the Petit Palais on the Avenue Winston-Churchill which, with the Avenue Marigny, provides an outlet to the Faubourg Saint-Honoré.

This splendid work, erected in only two years (1898-1900) was the last Parisian bridge of the 19th century, a century that had built or restored so many. It is the achievement of the engineers Resal and Alby and the architects Cassien-Bernard and Causin. The work was assigned to the major national steel companies, Schneider and Fives-Lille (the latter for the cast-iron sculpted decor). Its unique arch, which bears a pressure of 13,000 tons, represents a remarkable technical accomplishment.

President Félix Faure and Prime Minister Méline took advantage of the visit to Paris of Czar Nicholas II and Empress Alexandra Feodorovna to lay a first, ceremonial stone on October 7, 1896.

The decoration of the bridge, dominated by the marine mythology that the Belle Epoque loved (the masked balls of the period were populated by tritons, naiades, and other sea-monsters) was commissioned to a pleiad of sculptors: Frémiet, Michel, Granet, Coutan, Steiner, Poulin, Récipon, Morice, Massoule, Gauquic. The stone lions on the Left Bank (the Glory of War) are by Dalou, while those on the Right Bank (the Joy of Peace) are by Gardet.

The Pont des Invalides

Another Second Empire bridge, built in 1855-56, was completed a year late for the opening of the Exposition Universelle of May 1855.

It replaced a suspended bridge of 1829, called "Pont d'Antin," which was more original but less stable (chains were used instead of cables).

The present bridge has five arches, with the ones in the center three feet narrower than those on the side, the opposite of usual construction.

One of the two statues situated on the center pier, the Naval Victory, is the work of Georges Dieboldt, who made the "Zouave" of the Alma Bridge.

The Pont de l'Alma

This bridge is famous for its statue of a "Zouave" (French infantryman in the colonial army), a miraculous survivor of the former bridge. The Zouave, a statue by Georges Dieboldt, originally stood with three other soldiers guarding the bridge built in 1856 by architect Cariel and baptized in commemoration of the victory of the French and English troops over the Russians in the Crimean War (1854).

The 1856 bridge had been conceived as an outlet to the new quarter of Chaillot, which was then being developed. A century later, the bridge proved insufficient for the increasing traffic. Instead of widening it, as had been done elsewhere, it was completely destroyed in 1970-72. Together with the Halles, the Front de Seine, and the Montparnasse Tower, this demolition is another misdeed of a decade obsessed with modernity at any price. The present bridge rests on a single pier in the river; at one-fifth of its length on the Right Bank side in this pylon with the sole purpose of reestablishing the Zouave.

The Passerelle Debilly

Named after the General Debilly who was killed in the imperial battle of Iéna, the footbridge was built in 1900 to facilitate visiting the palaces of the Exposition Universelle, which spread over the two banks.

The elegant, metallic structure was designed by the engineers Lion, Alby, and Resal. It remains a pedestrian bridge linking the quais Branly (Left Bank) and New York (Right Bank) where the Museum of Modern Art stands.

The Pont d'Iéna

On the axis of the Eiffel Tower and the Chaillot Palace, a perspective rivalling the Invalides for monumentality, the Iéna bridge was constructed during 1806-13 according to the plans of Lamandé (engineer of the Austerlitz bridge).

Baptized by a decree of Napoleon from Warsaw in memory of the Iéna Victory (October 14, 1806), the bridge is made of five stone arches and has been enlarged twice, in

1914 and 1936. The four equestrian statues (Greek, Roman, Gallic, and Arab warriors) were installed in 1852.

These details, however, don't entirely explain J.F. Cooper's enthusiasm: "The Iéna Bridge is as close to perfection in all respects as a bridge can be. I like it much better than the famous Trinity Bridge in Florence."

The Pont Bir-Hakeim

This metallic bridge, together with the metro-viaduc that it bears, was built from 1903 to 1905. It aligns in the middle of the river on the island dubbed "of the swans" in memory of another island nearby that Louis XIV had populated with big white swans in 1676.

Above the piers, the groups of blacksmiths and tritons are by sculptor Gustave Michel.

The Bir-Hakeim Bridge (Passy Bridge until 1949) commemorates a victory of the Free France troops over Rommel's tanks in the Libyan desert (1942).

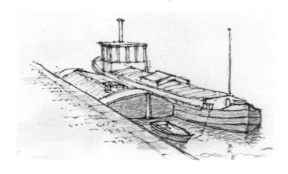

The Pont de Grenelle

This bridge links two periods of contemporary French architecture: the "Maison de la Radio" (1963) and, from a decade later, the towers of the "Front de Seine" which reflect the time when Paris sought to emulate American skyscrapers. Prophetically in 1885, a small-scale replica of the Statue of Liberty by Bartholdi was placed at the west-

ern tip of the Island of the Swans where the arches of the Grenelle Bridge meet. The statue was restored for the Centennial, at the same time as its counterpart in New York.

The present bridge dates to 1968 and replaced a cast-iron work built in 1874 by engineers Vaudrey and Pesson.

Pont Mirabeau

Erected between the popular quai André Citroën (Javel-Grenelle area on the Left Bank) and the fancy Auteuil quarter (Right Bank) in 1896, this bridge is the work of Resal, the engineer of the Alexandre III Bridge and the Debilly footbridge.

The French poet Guillaume Apollinaire once commented: "Pass the nights and pass the weeks, neither time past nor Love come back. Under the Mirabeau Bridge passes the Seine."

A propos des Ponts

Jean-Marie Besset

Pont-Neuf

Le plus célèbre des ponts de Paris est aussi celui qui a le mieux gardé son aspect d'origine. A quelques détails près, il est en cette fin de XXe siècle tel qu'il se présenta le 20 juin 1603 à Henri IV qui le traversa pour la première fois.

C'est au Second Empire que nous devons sa splendide restauration. Le pont, en effet, peu retouché depuis sa construction, tombait en ruine en 1848. La réparation générale permit de refaire en entier ses 12 arcades, les parements de têtes, les parapets et la corniche, ainsi que de supprimer les boutiques qui avaient été ajoutées en 1775 dans les demi-lunes appuyées sur les piles, qui donnent au Pont-Neuf son aspect si caractéristique. Le pont unit la rue Dauphine (rive gauche) à la rue de la Monnaie (rive droite), en trouvant un large appui sur la pointe de l'île de la Cité, derrière la place Dauphine.

Le développement de l'Université, l'accroissement du trafic, la fragilité des ponts au Change et Notre-Dame (surchargés par les maisons qu'ils portaient) rendaient nécessaire, au milieu du XVIe siècle, l'établissement d'un nouveau pont. Ce point de la ville entre le Louvre et l'Hôtel de Nesles étant devenu un coupe-gorge, du fait de la complicité entre les passeurs et les brigands qui détroussaient les Parisiens, on envisagea dès 1556, par mesure de salubrité publique, d'y construire le pont nécessaire.

Le 31 mai 1578, Henri III vint sur une barque magnifiquement ornée en poser la première pierre, accompagné de la reine mère, Catherine de Médicis. Malgré les efforts du jeune architecte du roi, Androuet du Cerceau, l'ouvrage ne put être terminé avant la guerre civile. Le roi pourtant s'intéressait à la construction et avait hâte de voir le pont achevé. Un hiver, il fit jeter un pont de bois d'une rive à l'autre sur les pierres des piles inachevées et traversa avec toute sa cour pour aller à une fête aux Grands-Augustins donnée en l'honneur de l'Ordre nouveau du Saint Esprit. Ce fut la seule fois qu'Henri III traversa "son" pont, qui ne fut achevé qu'après la guerre, sous Henri IV.

C'est la statue de ce dernier qui se trouva donc érigée sur ce pont, par ordre de son fils, Louis XIII, en 1614. La statue actuelle est une copie fondue sous le Second Empire de l'original, détruit sous la Révolution qui mit à sa place un drapeau tricolore.

Ce Pont-Neuf, le premier pont de Paris à avoir été construit sans maisons, devait aussitôt devenir le centre de la vie parisienne. Un proverbe assurait qu'on pouvait y voir, à toute heure du jour, un cheval blanc, une courtisane et un frocard (moine). En matière de cheval blanc, il y avait bien sûr la statue de celui d'Henri IV . . .

Pont Saint-Michel

On doit l'actuel pont Saint-Michel, comme le pont au Change qu'il prolonge, du boulevard du Palais (sur l'île) à la place Saint-Michel (rive gauche), au Second Empire. Egalement orné de "N" et lauriers, cet ouvrage en trois arches en moellons piqués réunis par du ciment de Portland (c'était une innovation) est l'œuvre de l'ingénieur Vaudrey.

Jusqu'à la fin du XIVᵉ siècle, le seul lien entre l'île de la Cité et la rive gauche était le Petit Pont. C'est en 1378 qu'on construisit le premier pont Saint-Michel, fini sous Charles VI en 1387 en employant "à l'ordinaire, ainsi qu'autres ouvrages publics, les vagabonds, les joueurs et les fainéans". La précision, d'un historien optimiste, distingue les trois catégories: elle suppose les joueurs industrieux, les fainéants sédentaires et les vagabonds peu enclins au jeu . . . Le pont Saint-Michel était né, ainsi nommé

d'après une chapelle qui se trouvait sur une petite place entre la Sainte-Chapelle et la rue Saint-Michel, où Philippe Auguste avait reçu le baptême, le 23 août 1165.

Petit Pont

Ainsi nommé, comme on a vu, par opposition au Grand Pont (aujourd'hui Notre-Dame) de l'époque romaine, le Petit Pont est resté, entre les quais de Montebello (rive gauche) et du Marché Neuf (sur l'île de la Cité), le plus court de Paris (40m). Fait d'une seule arche en meulière et ciment, il remplaça pour les commodités de la navigation un élégant ouvrage en trois arches du début du XVIIIᵉ siècle.

C'est à ce petit pont que nous devons l'origine d'une des plus curieuses de nos expressions: "Payer en monnaie de singe". En 1206 en effet, Louis IX (Saint Louis) fixa le tarif du péage à l'entrée de Paris sous le petit

Châtelet (sur l'île de la Cité) avec cette précision: "Le marchand qui apportera un singe pour le vendre à Paris payera 4 deniers d'entrée; que si ce singe appartient à un joculateur, cet homme en le faisant jouer et danser, le péage sera acquitté, tant dudit singe que de tout ce qu'il aura apporté pour son voyage."

Les péages de nos autoroutes n'ont pas de ces subtilités: barrières électroniques et cartes perforées se moquent de savoir à quoi, sur la banquette arrière, vous destinez votre quadrupède favori.

Pont-au-Double

La construction, au début du XVIIᵉ siècle, de nouveaux hôpitaux dans Paris ne parvenait pas à désencombrer l'Hôtel-Dieu. On résolut donc en 1626 de construire un pont destiné à supporter des salles de malades. A la demande des riverains, un passage

public fut ménagé (un tiers de la largeur du pont) qui permettait de passer du parvis de Notre-Dame à la rive gauche. Le péage en fut fixé sous Louis XIII à un double tournoi pour les cavaliers, d'où son nom.

Les embarras de circulation sur le pont et de navigation en dessous, la campagne pour la démolition des maisons sur les ponts de Paris furent cause de ce que le pont fut détruit et reconstruit plusieurs fois.

Comment imaginer, en voyant l'arc de fonte actuel (qui date de 1882) qu'il y eut à cet endroit, à la fin du Moyen-Age un pont de bois dit "pont-aux-ânes" en raison des bestiaux qui l'empruntaient pour aller paître dans les prairies qu'occupent aujourd'hui l'Entrepôt et le Jardin des Plantes?

Une farce du XVᵉ siècle met en scène un meunier de Gentilly, amoureux et jaloux, qui va consulter un célèbre docteur de la place Maubert sur le moyen de rendre son épouse moins volage. Il suit le conseil du médecin ("Allez sur le pont aux ânes") et il y voit, comme l'accotement du côté des prairies est rude et escarpé, les ânes qui l'escaladent avec difficulté recevoir des volées de coups de trique. Morale du temps:

"Nobles dames, qui avez soin
Vous pouvez par ceci noter
Le pont aux ânes est témoin
Besoin fait la vieille trotter".

Pont de l'Archevêché

Il relie la rive gauche et le quai de l'Archevêché à la hauteur du square Jean XXIII, cette pointe orientale de l'île de la Cité où, en 1407, Charlotte de Savoie, seconde femme de Louis XI, débarqua lors de son entrée à Paris.

Le pont fut commencé sous Charles X en avril 1828 et livré à la circulation dès novembre suivant: six mois pour cet ouvrage de maçonnerie en trois arches, voilà qui était une affaire rondement menée.

L'ancien palais épiscopal dont il tire son nom, sur le flanc de Notre-Dame, fut mis à sac et incendié le 15 février 1831 par des émeutiers vêtus en carnaval, enragés d'apprendre que les légitimistes faisaient célébrer une messe pour l'anniversaire de l'assassinat du duc de Berry.

Pont de la Tournelle

Il doit son nom à une tour carrée construite par Philippe Auguste pour défendre, avec la tour de Lauriot sur l'île Saint-Louis et la tour de Billy près des Célestins, sur la rive droite, l'entrée de Paris des deux côtés de la Seine.

La Tournelle, abandonnée, devait plus tard, à la requête de Saint Vincent de Paul, servir d'abri aux condamnés avant qu'ils ne fussent escortés à Marseille et affectés aux galères. La Tournelle fut une prison jusqu'en 1790.

On trouve dès le XIVe siècle trace d'un pont en bois, appelé "pont de fust de l'île Notre-Dame" qui reliait à la rive gauche.

Il fut reconstruit plusieurs fois, toujours en bois, notamment en 1620 par Christophe Marie, qui entendait favoriser les opérations de lotissement qu'il menait dans l'île.

A cause des inondations—fléau régulier dont nous avons perdu la mémoire—on décida au milieu du XVIIe siècle de construire un pont en pierre, de six arches en plein cintre.

Le pont actuel rend mal compte du caractère de l'ancien, bâti sous le roi Soleil. Il est en béton armé, avec têtes en pierre de taille composé d'une grande arche centrale et de deux latérales. Sa ligne est enlaidie par une sorte de fusée blanche, qui est en fait une Sainte Geneviève sur piédestal interminable par le sculpteur Landowski.

On voudrait dire de cette statue ce que Voltaire, dans les "Dialogues", disait des maisons: "On voyait avec indignation de très vilaines maisons sur de très beaux ponts".

Pont Sully

Il consiste en fait en deux ponts métalliques réalisés de 1874 à 1876 pour relier le boulevard Saint-Germain au boulevard Henri IV et à cheval sur l'île Saint-Louis où il n'y a plus aujourd'hui, outre la maison du glacier Bertillon, que les folies des écrivains et les pieds-à-terre des Américains.

"Les" ponts Sully coexistèrent jusqu'en 1933, entre la pointe amont de l'île et le quai Henri IV, avec une ancienne passerelle pour piétons sur estacade en bois. L'estacade protégeait de la dérive des glaces les bateaux garés au port des Célestins-Saint-Paul, sur le petit bras de la Seine. Protection fragile puisque l'estacade, quand elle ne brûlait pas, était couramment emportée par les glaces.

Lorsque la partie sud du pont fut construite, on découvrit rive gauche côté boulevard-Saint Germain, l'extrémité de l'enceinte de Philippe Auguste ainsi que les fondements du bâtiment de la Tournelle.

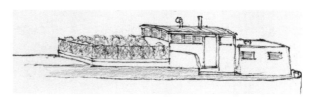

Pont d'Austerlitz

Un premier pont dessiné par l'ingénieur Becquey-Beaupré fut inauguré le 5 mars 1807 pour commémorer la victoire de l'Empereur du 2 décembre 1805. Il reliait les places Mazas et Valhubert, également nommées d'après deux militaires tombés au champ d'honneur d'Austerlitz. A considérer aujourd'hui la hideur des bâtiments du quai de la Rapée on est surpris de lire les gazettes de l'époque s'ébaubir de "la magnificence du site dans lequel il est jeté".

Le Second Empire voulant mettre ses ors à célébrer les guerres du Premier d'autant que les arches de fonte résistaient mal au trafic croissant entre les gares d'Orléans et de Lyon le pont de fer fut remplacé en 1855 par un pont de pierre. Le tablier en fut encore élargi en 1885, pour répondre à des besoins de circulation plus intenses.

Dans le taxi lancé sur le bitume à l'assaut, tel vendredi soir, du dernier train Paris-Port Bou, le méridional a du mal à se figurer le temps où, à la suggestion de M. le Comte de Buffon, directeur du jardin des Plantes, deux bacs remplacèrent ici les simples batelets qui transportaient les piétons d'une rive à l'autre. C'était en 1783 et la tyrannie du 23h02 était insoupçonnée.

Pont Marie

L'île Saint-Louis, autrefois île Notre-Dame, fut, à la fin du treizième siècle, un des hauts lieux d'où l'on prêcha la croisade. Elle resta longtemps sans communiquer avec l'île de la Cité et les rives de la Seine. Des ponts ne s'imposaient guère car l'île était inhabitée, partagée en deux par un grand fossé (on aurait dit deux îles: "les îles Notre-Dame") qui rendait le terrain pentu et peu propice à la construction.

Le 19 avril 1614, un acte de Louis XIII autorisa l'entrepreneur Christophe Marie à combler le fossé et à établir à ses frais un pont de pierre pour faire communiquer le quartier Saint-Paul et celui de la Tournelle. En échange de son pont, le rusé Christophe Marie obtenait "délaissements en fonds et propriété à perpétuité que lui fait Sa Majesté des deux îles Notre-Dame". L'affaire était plutôt bonne, et il semble qu'en matière de spéculation immobilière, ledit Marie fut un pionnier. Le pont fut achevé en 1635.

Marie avait également obtenu de "faire construire sur le pont des maisons toutes d'une même symétrie et élévation, à la charge d'y laisser quatre toises de rue pour servir au public". La terrible inondation qui submergea la moitié de Paris en février-mars 1658 emporta la moitié du pont. On incrimina la lourdeur des maisons et les malheureux habitants des logis épargnés se virent menacés d'expulsion en 1666. D'autant qu'en 1670, les deux arches emportées furent rétablies sans maisons au-dessus. L'expulsion était, alors comme aujourd'hui, chose délicate à faire exécuter, d'autant qu'il s'agissait en l'espèce de propriétaires légitimes. L'inondation de 1740 dépassa en violence celle de 1658: "C'est pleine rivière, de tous les côtés on est réfugié à l'étage. Tous les habitants de l'île Notre-Dame sont enfermés", rapporte un témoin.

Les magistrats prirent enfin des mesures exceptionnelles et proclamèrent l'édit de 1741 prescrivant la destruction de toutes les maisons sur les ponts de Paris.

Les dernières maisons du pont Marie ne furent cependant abattues qu'en . . . 1788, libérant la perspective sur la Seine et le Paris de la Révolution.

Pont Louis-Philippe

Louis Philippe Ier, en présence de Monsieur Thiers, ministre, et du Comte de Rambuteau, préfet, inaugura en juillet 1834 un pont reliant le quai de la Grève—rive droite—à l'île de la Cité, suspendu à un portique planté sur la pointe ouest de l'île Saint-Louis. La partie suspendue entre les deux îles rendait superflue la passerelle de la Cité (aujourd'hui pont Saint Louis), située juste à côté.

Le pont fut rebaptisé "de la Réforme" dans 1'enthousiasme de 1848. Ce nouveau nom fut plus éphémère que la IIe République et que le pont lui-même, détruit par un feu qui fit rompre ses chaînes et tomber toute la travée dans la Seine.

Reconstruit en pierre et sur un modèle plus traditionnel en 1860, il reprit sous l'empereur le nom du roi des Français.

C'est tout dire de cet ouvrage de maçonnerie en trois arches qu'il coûta 576.008 francs et 58 centimes. Pas un sou de plus.

Pont Saint-Louis

Christophe Marie, maître d'œuvre des travaux de l'île Saint-Louis (alors Notre Dame) et qui avait relié "son" île aux rives droite (pont Marie) et gauche (pont de la Tournelle) obtint de construire un pont de bois pour que les insulaires de ses lotissements puissent aller faire leurs dévotions à pied, sans faire de détours par les berges. Le chapître de Notre-Dame s'y opposa longtemps, avant de se laisser benoîtement convaincre: le chapître avait gagné en échange le libre usage de 30 pieds de quai du port Saint-Landry voisin et la promesse que ni les chanoines ni leurs domestiques ne paieraient le péage d'un liard, institué par Christophe Marie qui, décidément, avait le sens des affaires.

Le 5 juin 1634, trois processions voulurent passer ensemble pour se rendre à Notre Dame et le pont manqua céder. Bilan, 20 morts et 40 blessés, comme on dit aujourd' hui lorsque telle tribune de nos stades vient à s'effondrer sous le poids des supporters. Deux ans plus tard, en prévision des foules du Jubilé, on construisit deux barrières de bois à chaque entrée de pont.

Le succès de l'île et de ses ponts dépassait les espoirs de Christophe Marie, qui s'il avait vécu, eût fini assurément par inventer . . . le Club Méditerranée.

En 1710, on construisit un nouveau pont en bois, dit pont "rouge" à cause de la peinture au minium qui devait protéger le bois de l'humidité. Un témoin du temps se moquait de "cette construction bizarre et ridicule qui fait honte à Paris où tout devrait paraître solide et magnifique" (G. Brice). L'arrêt de cet homme des Lumières pourrait aussi bien s'appliquer au stupide pont actuel, qui a fini par remplacer, en 1970, une passerelle provisoire de 1941 installée à la suite de l'accident survenu à l'arche métallique construite sous Napoléon III.

Cette arche composée de neuf arcs de fonte eut en effet le malheur de se trouver sur le passage d'une péniche de 800 tonnes, qui l'envoya par le fond en décembre 1939. Un pont sur lequel les Allemands ne passeraient pas . . .

Pont d'Arcole

Napoléon, qui entendait asseoir six mille convives à sa table, les jours de réception à l'Hôtel de Ville, souhaitait que la place de Grève, agrandie, fut mise en communication avec Notre-Dame par un pont triomphal. Ces beaux projets, échaffaudés pendant les Cent Jours (1815) ne purent se réaliser, en raison des évènements que l'on sait.

Une passerelle, ouvrage modeste, fut construite à cet endroit en 1828, baptisée pont de Grève, du nom que portait alors le quai (rive droite) qui bordait l'Hôtel de Ville.

C'est du pont de Grève que, le 28 juillet 1830 (la cadette des "Trois Glorieuses") le peuple attaqua la troupe qui défendait l'Hôtel de Ville au cri de "Vive la Charte". Un jeune homme, drapeau à la main, s'élança à la tête d'un groupe de républicains sur le pont balayé par le tir des gendarmes et tomba en criant quelque chose où on entendit le mot "Arcole". Etait-

ce son nom? Invoquait-il la victoire italienne de l'Empereur? Toujours est-il que le pont fut baptisé d'Arcole en mémoire de l'intrépide citoyen.

Les grands travaux menés par Haussmann, en dégageant les abords de l'Hôtel de Ville, rendirent nécessaire un pont plus important. Le 15 octobre 1855, un pont de fer en une arche, dessiné par l'ingénieur Oudry, fut ouvert à la circulation. La Commune et la Libération de Paris (âout 1944) devaient encore faire couler du sang sur ce pont stratégique.

Pont Notre-Dame

Le pont actuel a été construit en 1853, à l'époque du percement de la rue de Rivoli à son croisement avec la rue Saint Martin. Des cinq voûtes du pont de 1853, les trois centrales ont été remplacées en 1912 par une seule arche métallique, moins génante pour la navigation.

Dès l'époque romaine, on trouve à cet emplacement névralgique une passerelle en bois dite Grand Pont. Lutèce (l'actuelle île de la Cité) était en effet reliée aux rives de la Seine par deux ponts, l'un, dit "Grand", jeté sur le grand bras (côté rive droite), l'autre appelé "Petit Pont" (côté rive gauche). Au Moyen-Age, les deux ponts traçaient un axe parfait Nord-Sud, de la Porte Saint-Martin à la porte Saint-Jacques, en passant, sur l'île, dans l'alignement des rues de la Lanterne, de la Juiverie et du marché Palu.

En 1406, le pont de la planche de Mibray (de "mi-bras": la moitié du bras de la Seine), successeur du Grand Pont romain, fut emporté par les inondations. Un historien du temps rapporte que: "Les habitants firent une collecte pour le faire rétablir, et en déposèrent le produit à l'Hôtel de Ville. Malheureusement, les Echevins mangèrent le pont. Il fallut plaider, leur faire rendre gorge et les pauvres Parisiens se passèrent de

leur pont central pendant douze ans". Le mercredi 31 mai 1413, le roi vint inaugurer le nouveau pont de bois, et le baptisa du nom de Notre-Dame.

Un siècle plus tard, le pont fut rebâti en pierre et inauguré en fanfare le 10 juillet 1507. Le pont arborait 68 belles maisons semblables (34 de chaque côté), "toutes marquées de lettres d'or sur fond rouge", ce qui passe pour le premier essai de numérotation des rues en France.

L'Anglais Thomas Coryate décrit à l'époque cette rue du pont Notre-Dame comme la plus belle de Paris: "Sous un rapport, elle surpasse toutes les rues de Londres: ses maisons sont complètement uniformes; elles sont construites sur un même plan et avec les mêmes matériaux". Venant d'un habitant de la future cité des "crescents", le compliment était sincère.

Pont-au-Change

Il relia longtemps deux prisons: la Conciergerie et le Châtelet. L'une devenue musée et l'autre théâtre. Le pont actuel a été, comme la plupart des ponts de Paris, reconstruit par Haussmann en 1859-60 afin d'être placé dans l'alignement du nouveau boulevard du Palais (sur l'île), tracé à la même èpoque, et de la place du Châtelet (rive droite) réaménagée.

Les trois arches ont été construites en moellons provenant de la retaille des pierres du pont précédent, bâti au milieu du XVIIe siècle par Jacques Androuet du Cerceau. La ligne simple et majestueuse du pont se trouve rehaussée, au dessus de chaque pile, par une initiale entourée d'une couronne de lauriers: hommage en bas relief rendu au "N" majuscule par Napoléon le Petit.

Aux XIIIe et XIVe siècles, les maisons du pont étaient habitées par les changeurs et les orfèvres, d'où son nom. Par une ordonnance de 1304 en effet, Philippe le Bel y avait transféré le change du Grand Pont, alors détruit par les inondations.

Au XVIIe siècle, divers commerces de luxe y cotoyaient les orfèvres. Le mardi et le samedi matin en revanche s'y tenait le marché d'arbres et de fleurs (passé aujourd'hui sur l'île) et le dimanche, celui des volatiles (dont les odeurs animent à présent le quai de la Mégisserie sur la rive droite).

Pont des Arts

Il vient d'être reconstruit. Il fut réouvert aux piétons en 1985, quelques mois trop tard pour que les badauds puissent venir contempler du milieu de la Seine l'emballage du Pont-Neuf par l'artiste Christo, empaquetage et succès géants, qui usèrent la salive des Français et l'encre des journalistes presqu'autant que, l'année suivante, les colonnes de Buren érigées dans la cour du Palais-Royal.

Construit de 1802 à 1804, il était composé à l'origine de 9 arches en fonte (8 en 1852) reposant sur des piles en maçonnerie. Jusqu'à sa démolition en 1981, la passerelle restait l'exemple le plus ancien d'architecture métallique qu'on pouvait voir à Paris.

On ne sait plus si ce pont piétonnier fut baptisé des Arts parce qu'il se trouvait en face d'une des portes du Louvre (ex-Palais des Arts) ou parce qu'il aboutissait au Collège des Quatre-Nations où le Premier Consul voulait alors installer l'école des Beaux-Arts.

La splendide restauration de la cour carrée du Louvre, les foules qu'elle attire, redonnent un regain de fréquentation au pont des Arts, cher à Brassens:
"Si par hasard
Sur l'pont des Arts
Tu crois' le vent, le vent maraud
Prudence, prends garde à ton chapeau".

Le poète mourut en 1981, la même année que le pont des Arts original.

Pont du Carrousel

La version actuelle du pont du Carrousel, qui joint le quai Voltaire (près de la rue des Saints Pères) à la partie centrale du Louvre (où se trouve l'Arc de triomphe du même nom) date de 1939. Il est en béton recouvert de pierres de parement.

Il a remplacé le pont original (1834) dû à l'ingénieur Antoine-Rémy Polonceau, inventeur d'un procédé qui avait permis une ingénieuse construction en trois arches de fonte de 48 mètres d'ouverture. De ce précédent ouvrage subsistent seulement, aux extrémités, quatre statues de Petitôt, représentant l'Abondance et l'Industrie, la Seine et la Ville de Paris (1846).

Le pont commémore la fête de 1662 où, sur un vaste espace aménagé face au Louvre,

Louis XIV offrit à Melle de la Vallière un magnifique Carrousel: des gradins pour 15 000 spectateurs entouraient une piste où cinq quadrilles se déployèrent avec 10 chevaliers chacun, en costumes romains, persans, indiens, turcs et "américains".

Pont-Royal

Construit de 1685 à 1689 et seulement restauré en 1839, le Pont Royal est, avec le Pont-Neuf et le Pont Marie, l'un des trois anciens ponts de Paris. Son classement monument historique l'a protégé de la destruction préconisée maintes fois, au motif qu'il ne coïncide avec aucun axe, aboutissant rive droite au pied du pavillon de Flore (Louvre) et rive gauche devant des hôtels particuliers entre les rues du Bac et de Beaune.

En conséquence, il est raccordé avec les quais au moyen de pans coupés qui partent en biais du milieu des arches de rive, ce qui facilite beaucoup la circulation.

Offert à Paris par Louis XIV (d'où son nom), ouvrage du fameux architecte Mansart, le Pont-Royal avait remplacé un pont de bois détruit plusieurs fois et qui avait porté des noms divers. La dernière appellation de "pont rouge" (il était recouvert de peinture au minium) fut immortalisée lors des inondations de 1684 par un trait de Madame de Sévigné: "Le Pont-Rouge partait pour Saint-Cloud".

Composé de 5 arches en plein cintre, de ligne nette et de robuste apparence, le nouveau pont ne risquait pas un si ridicule voyage: "On y a négligé les ornements mais la solidité qu'on lui a donné promet une durée dont on ne verra pas la fin".

Au XVIIIe siècle, le Pont-Royal fut la tribune d'où on assistait aux grandes fêtes nautiques qui avaient lieu sur la Seine jusqu'au Pont-Neuf: celles d'août 1739 en l'honneur du mariage d'Elisabeth de France avec Don Philippe, infant d'Espagne, rassemblèrent sur les quais 500 000 personnes.

Pont Solferino

En face du jardin des Tuileries (rive droite), le pont Solferino a été décrété le 26 juillet 1858, inauguré le 14 août 1859 et baptisé d'après la victoire de Solferino (25 juin 1859), l'ensemble, défaite des Autrichiens comprise, par Napoléon III. Ce pont métallique en 3 arches nécessita 1200 tonnes de fonte.

Démoli en 1959, il n'est toujours pas remplacé, sinon par une passerelle provisoire. Un pont qui aboutit au double obstacle de la voie express et de la terrasse des Tuileries est une affaire délicate. En matière de construction de ponts, le Paris du XXe siècle paraît aussi pingre que dénué d'imagination. Peut-on juger le dynamisme d'une ville à la manière dont elle envisage ses ponts?

Pont de la Concorde

Pont symbolique qui unit l'Ancien Régime (la place de la Concorde s'appelait Louis XV) et le nouveau (Assemblée Nationale) et dont la construction se poursuivit en pleine Révolution.

A la fin du XVIII° siècle, les faubourgs Saint-Germain (rive gauche) et Saint-Honoré (rive droite) se peuplaient d'hôtels particuliers et il devenait urgent de jeter un pont entre la place Louis XV et la naissance du boulevard Saint-Germain.

Un édit de Louis XVI ordonne sa construction. L'ouvrage est confié à l'ingénieur Perronet (1708-1794), fondateur de l'Ecole Nationale des Ponts et Chaussées, qui innove en réduisant l'épaisseur des piles et en adoptant des voûtes très surbaissées. Les travaux s'étendent sur trois ans, de 1788 à 1791 et la première pierre posée (11 août 88) est évidemment d'une nature différente des autres, qui viendront de la Bastille dé-

truite, "afin que le peuple puisse continuellement fouler aux pieds l'antique forteresse".

Il a été doublé en largeur en 1930-32, travaux bien menés qui ont heureusement gardé le profil du pont de Perronet.

Pont Alexandre III

Dans l'axe qui va du dôme des Invalides aux Champs-Elysées, le plus beau des ponts de Paris est un des trois éléments d'une perspective monumentale avec l'esplanade des Invalides et l'avenue Winston-Churchill entre le Grand et le Petit Palais (qui forme avec l'avenue Marigny un débouché au Faubourg Saint-Honoré).

L'ouvrage, érigé en 2 ans seulement (1898-1900) fut le dernier pont parisien du XIX° siècle qui en avait tant construits ou restaurés. Il est l'œuvre des ingénieurs Resal et Alby et des architectes Cassien-Bernard et Causin. Les travaux furent confiés aux deux grands de la sidérurgie nationale: Schneider (usine du Creusot) et Fives-Lille

pour le décor sculpté en fonte moulée. Son arche unique, qui fait supporter une poussée de 13 000 tonnes sur les culées, constitue une prouesse technique.

On profita de la visite à Paris du Tsar Nicolas II et de l'impératrice Alexandra Féodorovna pour poser la première pierre, le 7 octobre 1896, en présence du Président de la République, M. Félix Faure, et de M. Méline, président du Conseil.

La décoration du pont, dominée par des mythologies marines dont la Belle Epoque était friande (les bals masqués témoignent d'un imaginaire peuplé de tritons, naïades et autres monstres marins) fut confiée à une pléiade de sculpteurs: Frémiet, Michel, Granet, Coutan, Steiner, Poulin, Récipon, Morice, Massoule, Gauquic. Notons enfin que si les lions de pierre de la rive gauche (la Gloire de la guerre) sont de Dalou, ceux de la rive droite (la Joie de la paix) sont de Gardet.

Pont des Invalides

Encore un pont du Second Empire, bâti en 1855-56, livré avec un an de retard sur la date de l'Exposition Universelle de mai 1855.

Il a remplacé un pont suspendu de 1829, dit Pont d'Antin, plus original mais à la stabilité précaire (on suspendait avec des chaînes et non avec des câbles). Le pont actuel est en 5 arches, celles du centre de près d'un mètre plus étroites que celles des côtés, contrairement à ce qui se pratique d'ordinaire.

Sur la pile centrale sont assises deux statues, Victoire terrestre et Victoire maritime; cette dernière est l'œuvre de Georges Dieboldt, l'homme du zouave du pont de l'Alma.

Pont de l'Alma

Il est fameux pour son zouave, rescapé miraculeux du pont antérieur. Le zouave est en effet une statue de Georges-Dieboldt qui, avec un grenadier, un chasseur et un artilleur (les deux derniers par Arnaud), montaient la garde auprès du pont construit par l'architecte Cariel en 1856, baptisé en commémoration de la victoire des Franco-Anglais sur les Russes en Crimée (1854).

Le pont de 1856 avait été conçu comme un débouché au nouveau quartier de Chaillot, alors en construction. Un siècle plus tard, le pont s'avérait insuffisant face au trafic automobile croissant. Au lieu de l'élargir, comme on a fait ailleurs, on le détruisit purement et simplement en 1970-72. Avec les Halles, le front de Seine et la tour Montparnasse, c'est là un autre méfait d'une décennie obnubilée par une politique à tout prix de la modernité. Le pont actuel est une structure métallique prenant appui sur une seule pile en rivière, au cinquième de sa longueur du côté de la rive droite: pile instituée à seule fin de réinstaller … le zouave.

Passerelle Debilly

Nommée en mémoire du général Debilly tué dans la bataille impériale d'Iéna, elle fut construite en 1900 pour faciliter la visite des palais de l'Exposition Universelle, qui occupait les deux rives.

Elégante charpente métallique dessinée par les ingénieurs Lion, Alby et Résal, elle est demeurée piétonne, entre les quais Branly (rive gauche) et de New-York (rive droite) où se dresse le musée d'art moderne.

Pont d'Iéna

Dans l'axe de la Tour Eiffel et du palais de Chaillot, perspective aussi monumentale que celle des Invalides, le pont d'Iéna fut édifié de 1806 à 1813 selon les plans de Lamandé (l'ingénieur du pont d'Austerlitz).

Baptisé par un décret de l'Empereur, daté de Varsovie, en mémoire de la victoire d'Iéna (14 octobre 1806), le pont est composé de 5 arches en pierre et a été élargi deux fois, en 1914 et en 1936. Les quatre statues équestres des extrémités (guerriers grec, romain, gaulois et arabe) ont été installées en 1852.

Ces détails n'expliquent cependant pas l'enthousiasme de James Fenimore Cooper: "Le pont d'Iéna est aussi voisin de la perfection sous tous ses rapports qu'un pont peut l'être. Je le préfère de beaucoup au célèbre pont de la Trinité à Florence."

Pont Bir-Hakeim

Ce pont métallique, de même que le viaduc du métropolitain qu'il supporte, a été édifié de 1903 à 1905. Il s'appuie au milieu du fleuve sur l'île dite des Cygnes en mémoire d'une île voisine que Louis XIV, en 1676, peupla de grands cygnes blancs "pour embellir la rivière de Seine".

Au-dessus des piles, enchevêtrés dans les colonnes métalliques, les ensembles de forgerons et tritons sont l'œuvre du sculpteur Gustave Michel.

Le pont Bir-Hakeim (de Passy jusqu'en 1949) commémore une victoire des troupes de la France Libre sur les blindés de Rommel dans le désert de Lybie (1942).

Pont de Grenelle

Il réunit aujourd'hui deux époques de l'architecture française contemporaine: la Maison de la Radio (1963) et, à dix ans de distance, les tours du front de Seine qui datent du temps où Paris voulait ses buildings américains à elle.

Signe avant-coureur, une réplique de la statue de la Liberté de Bartholdi, réduction de celle de New-York, se dresse depuis 1885 à la pointe ouest de l'île des Cygnes où s'appuient les deux arches du pont de Grenelle. La statue a été réparée pour les fêtes du centenaire, en même temps que sa grande jumelle de New-York.

Le pont actuel date de 1968 et a remplacé un ouvrage de fonte construit en 1874, œuvre des ingénieurs Vaudrey et Pesson.

Pont Mirabeau

Jeté en 1896 entre le populaire quai André Citroën (quartier de Javel-Grenelle sur la rive gauche) et les beaux quartiers d'Auteuil (rive droite), il est l'œuvre de Résal, l'ingénieur du pont Alexandre III et de la passerelle Debilly.

A quelle aventure amoureuse cet ouvrage métallique en trois arches, orné de dieux marins en bronze, doit-il la gloire que lui a accordé Apollinaire?

"Passent les nuits et passent les
    semaines
Ni temps passé
Ni les Amours reviennent
Sous le pont Mirabeau coule la Seine."

Artist's Note

In 1969 I began what I hoped would be the crowning project of my life. But how to draw? Should I use the basic method over a long stretch of time, standing on the verge of throbbing traffic to get the "feel" of the site, regardless of certain danger from traffic but clear of the irritations and interruptions of onlookers? Should I try to develop a "new way" for me to draw and if possible invent an entirely new technique? Even though the "new way" would not be applicable to the Paris series, perhaps I could use it later or, better still, stimulate someone else to perfect a new and brilliant technique.

Thus began two years of experimentation with carbon pencil, both black and terracotta, and with fountain pen ink, for doing the basic drawing, then using different types of brushes with varying degrees of wetness to brush over pen or carbon pencil lines. These experiments indicated the rich variations possible, depending upon the interaction of paper texture, wetness of brush, and degree of opacity of ink or carbon pencil. The blurring of line often suggested the movement of tree branches, persons, or vehicles; it seemed to offer potential "newness" in drawing effects. However, eventually I realized that sometimes the excessive wetness of the brush ruined the basic drawing, and if this were done "on location," it would have required beginning all over again with a new drawing. Nor could I follow my preference of doing all work standing up because of a rather complicated kit of water and brushes, which called for a multiplicity of arms. It was one thing to theorize in my New Canaan workroom, and another to actually draw in typical Paris locations. So it was that I finally settled for drawing with a standard graphite pencil and making copious notes so that I could develop the street sketches into finalized drawings at home in my workroom.

While in Paris during 1969 and 1970, I took many photos and notes on the best

sites for the best compositions. Being on my feet most of the day, it became apparent that if I were to succeed in producing drawings which were "fresh" rather than "tired," I would have to be "in training." My plan was to leave our hotel each day not later than 9:30 a.m., meet my wife for a picnic lunch somewhere along the Seine, resume drawing immediately after lunch, and not return to the hotel until about 4:30, having been walking from one drawing site to another or, more enervating, standing still for several hours drawing.

My pre-Paris training began in New Canaan about a month before our departure. Gradually I would work up to the equivalent in energy consumption of a day's sketching in Paris. I would leave our home about 9:30 a.m. armed with the drawing kit and materials, walk to Meade Park near the center of New Canaan, find a good composition to draw standing up, then about noon walk home for a lunch comparable to what

we would have sitting on a bench overlooking the Seine. After lunch, without any relaxation, I would walk with drawing kit to the Waveny Estate, about a mile away, and draw there standing up until about 4 p.m.

The four-year program from 1971 to 1975 was repetitive. I drew in Paris the entire month of September, when the weather is usually stable and our favorite restaurants are open again after the August hiatus. The balance of the year I spent in my workroom, developing finished drawings from the Paris sketches, designing suitable sky effects to connote historical crises or appropriate atmospheric moods.

G.K.G.

PARIS ALONG THE SEINE • GERALD K. GEERLINGS

A- Quai du Louvre   1- Pont des Arts   2- Palais du Louvre   3- Place du Louvre   B- Quai de Conti, lower level

The Quai du Louvre as viewed looking north across the Seine to the Quai de Conti

1-Square du Vert Gallant / 2-Statue of Henri IV / 3-Place Dauphine / 4-Spire of Ste. Chapelle / 5-South Tower, Palais de Justice
(little park, west end of Île de la Cité
A-Quai de Conti

The Ile de la Cité as viewed from the Quai de Conti

Left Bank Right Bank Île de la Cité

A-Quai des Grands Augestins   1-Louvre   2-Statue of Henri IV   B-Quai des Orfèrres

The Pont-Neuf as viewed from the Left Bank

1-South Tower of Palais de Justice   2-Place St. Michel

A-Quai des Orfèvres   B- Quai du Marché Neuf   C- Quai St. Michel   D- Quai des Grands Augustins

The Pont Saint-Michel as viewed from the Left Bank

A-Quai St. Michel   1-Place St. Michel   B - Quai des Grands Augustins

The Pont Saint-Michel as viewed from the Ile de la Cité looking toward the Left Bank

1-Place St. Michel   2-Grand Palais and Petit Palais   3-South Tower of Palais de Justice

A-Quai St. Michel   B- Quai des Grand Augustins   C- Quai du Marché Neuf

The Pont Saint-Michel as viewed from the Petit Pont

Gerald K. Geerlings

1 - Rue de la Huchette   2 - Préfecture de Police on further side of Seine.

A - Quai St. Michel   1 - Rue de la Huchette

View looking north toward the Quai Saint-Michel
and the Quai du Marché Neuf

View from the Quai du Marché Neuf, looking
across Seine to the Quai Saint-Michel

A- Quai du Marché Neuf   1- Nôtre Dame / 2- Place du Parvis Nôtre Dame   B- Quai St. Michel
3- Arch of Pont St. Michel

The Petit Pont from below the Left Bank end of the Pont Saint-Michel

Left Bank

N

1-St. Julien-le-Pauvre, across Seine from Nôtre Dame / 2-Acacia planted circa 1681 / 3- U-shape, concrete support

Gerett K. Geerlings

Saint-Julien-le-Pauvre on the Square René-Viviani looking south from the Quai de Montebello

50

A-Quai de Montebello / 1-Hôtel Dieu / 2-Nôtre Dame / 3-Trunk-shaped, concrete support / 4-U-shaped, concrete support

The Square René-Viviani

1-Square René Viviani / 2-Grand Palais / 3-South Tower of Palais de Justice / 4-Place du Parvis Nôtre Dame
A- Quai de Montebello

The Petit Pont from the Pont-au-Double

Notre-Dame viewed from the Petit Pont

Île de la Cité — Left Bank — N E W S

1-Nôtre Dame / 2-Place du Parvis Nôtre Dame / 3-Pont de l'Archêveché / A - Quai de Montebello

The Pont-au-Double as viewed from the Petit Pont

Île de la Cité   Left Bank

1-Pont au Double / 2-Statue of Charlemagne / 3-Place du Parvis Nôtre Dame / 4-Square René Viviani (on other side of Seine)

The Place du Parvis Notre-Dame looking toward the Left Bank

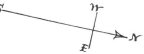

A-Quai de l'Archêreché / 1-South Tower of Palais de Justice / 2-Petit Pont / 3-Pont St. Michel / 4-Nôtre Dame / B-Quai de Montebello

The Pont-au-Double viewed from the Quai de Montebello on the Left Bank

Île de la Cité (forground)　　Île St. Louis (background)　　Left Bank

A - Quai l'Archevêché　　　　1 - Pont de la Tournelle　　　　B - Quai de Montebello

The Pont de l'Archevêché viewed from the lower level Quai on the Left Bank

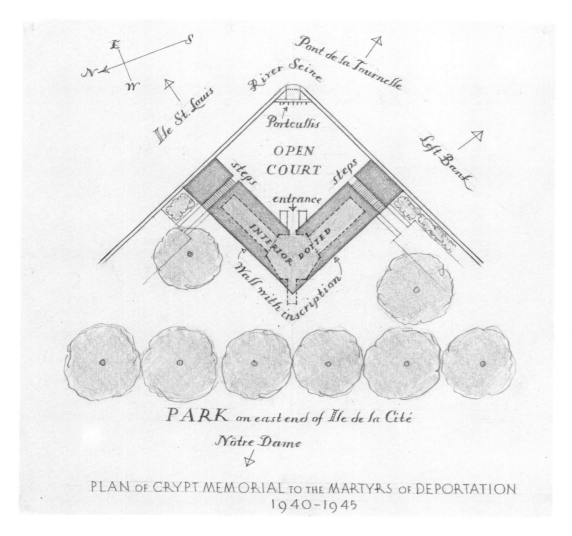

N E S W

Pont de la Tournelle

Ile St. Louis

River Seine

Left Bank

Portcullis

OPEN COURT

steps   steps

entrance

INTERIOR DOTTED

Wall with inscription

PARK on east end of Ile de la Cité

Nôtre Dame

PLAN OF CRYPT MEMORIAL TO THE MARTYRS OF DEPORTATION
1940-1945

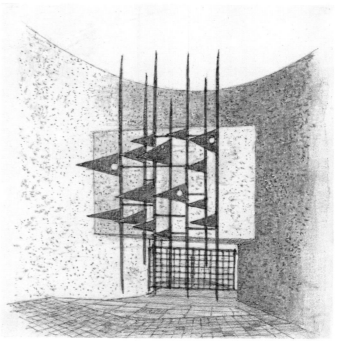

Interior court with symbolic portcullis, looking
southeast through grille toward Seine

The Crypte Mémorial and the symbolic portcullis

1-Stairs down to Crypte Mémorial / 2-Sq. de l'Île de France / 3-Pont de la Tournelle / 4-La Tour d'Argent restaurant

A - Quai d'Orléans   B - Quai de la Tournelle

The Crypte Mémorial viewed from the Square de l'Ile-de-France, looking toward the Port de la Tournelle

Île de la Cité

1-Spire of Nôtre Dame   2-Entrance to Interior of Memorial

Open courtyard of the Crypte Mémorial looking west

1–200,000 light facets / 2–Tomb of Unown Deportee / 3–Light in bronze floor plaque

The interior of the Crypte Mémorial

1-Pont de l'Archechêveche / 2-Notre Dame / 3-Memorial to French Jews killed by Nazis in World War II / 4-Pont St.Louis / 5-Pont d'Arcole / 6-Tour St.Jacques

A-Port de la Tournelle   B-Quai de l'Hotel de Ville / C-Quai d'Orleans / 7-Hotel de Ville

The Pont de l'Archevêché and the Pont Saint-Louis viewed from the Port de la Tournelle on the Left Bank

1 - Pont St. Louis

Notre-Dame viewed from the Quai d'Orléans on the Ile Saint-Louis

S W E N Left Bank | Île de la Cité | Île St. Louis

A – Pont de la Tournelle   1 – Statue: Ste. Geneviève   2 – Nôtre Dame   B – Quai de Béthune

The Pont de la Tournelle viewed from the Pont Sully

Île de la Cité   N   Île St. Louis

A—Quai de la Tournelle / 1—Pont de l'Archevêché / 2—Patron saint of Paris: Ste. Geneviève / B— Quai d'Orléans

The Pont de la Tournelle viewed from the Left Bank looking toward the Ile Saint-Louis

Île St. Louis — Buildings on Right Bank behind Île St. Louis park — Left Bank

Trees on Île St. Louis park

A—Quai de Béthune   1—Pont d'Austerlitz   B—Port St. Bernard

The Pont Sully viewed from the Pont de la Tournelle

66

Île St. Louis   Right Bank

Little park at east end of Île St. Louis

A-Port St. Bernard   1-Left Bank arm of Pont Sully / 2-Right Bank arm of Pont Sully / B-Quai Henri IV

East end of the Ile Saint-Louis viewed from the Left Bank

S · W · E · N

Left Bank — Île de la Cité — Île St. Louis — Right Bank

1-Ste. Geneviève statue on Pont de la Tournelle / 2-Nôtre Dame / 3-Pont de la Tournelle / 4-Left Bank spans of Pont Sully / 5-Right Bank spans of Pont Sully

A-Quai St. Bernard / B-Port St. Bernard

C-Port Henri IV

The Pont Sully with the Ile Saint-Louis between its two spans

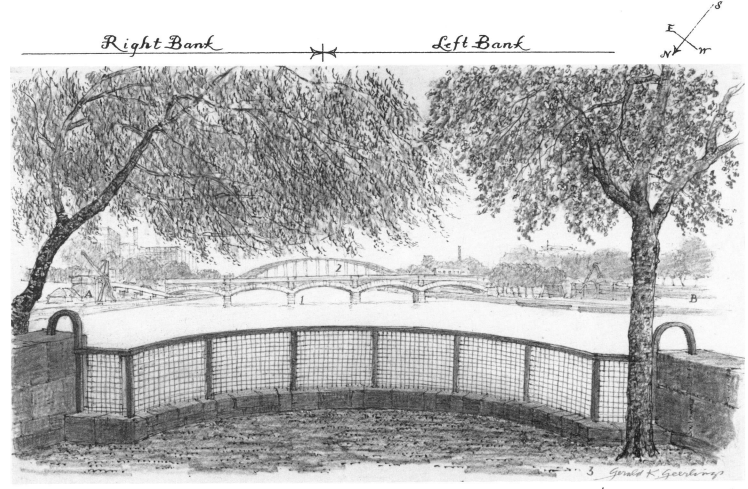

Right Bank ⊕ Left Bank

A-Port Henri IV / 1-Pont d'Austerlitz / 2-Railroad viaduc d'Austerlitz / 3- East end of Île St. Louis / B -Port St. Bernard

Looking east from the Ile Saint-Louis

N

A - Quai St. Bernard   1-Pont d'Austerlitz

Looking east from the Jardin des Plantes

Left Bank   Île St.Louis   Right Bank

A–Quai d'Austerlitz / B–Port d'Austerlitz   1–Pont Sully between Île St.Louis and Right Bank   C–Quai de la Rapée

The Pont d'Austerlitz viewed from the Port d'Austerlitz on the Left Bank

A-Quai des Célestins   B-Quai Henri IV   C-Quai d'Anjou

The Pont Sully viewed from the Right Bank

Île St. Louis | Left Bank in distance | Right Bank | N

A - Quai d'Anjou on Île St. Louis / B - Quai des Célestins (Right Bank) / 1 - Pont Marie   PLAN

The Pont Marie viewed from the Square Henri-Galli

A-Quai des Celestins   1-Pont Sully (Right Bank arm)   2-Hôtel de Lauzun   B-Quai d'Anjou

The Hôtel de Lauzun on the Ile Saint-Louis viewed from the Right Bank

A - Quai des Célestins   1 - Hôtel de Lauzun   B - Quai d'Anjou

The Right Bank viewed from the Ile Saint-Louis

A - Quai d'Anjou   1 - Pont Louis-Philippe with Pont d'Arcole beyond   B - Quai des Célestins

The Pont Marie viewed from the Quai Henri IV on the Right Bank

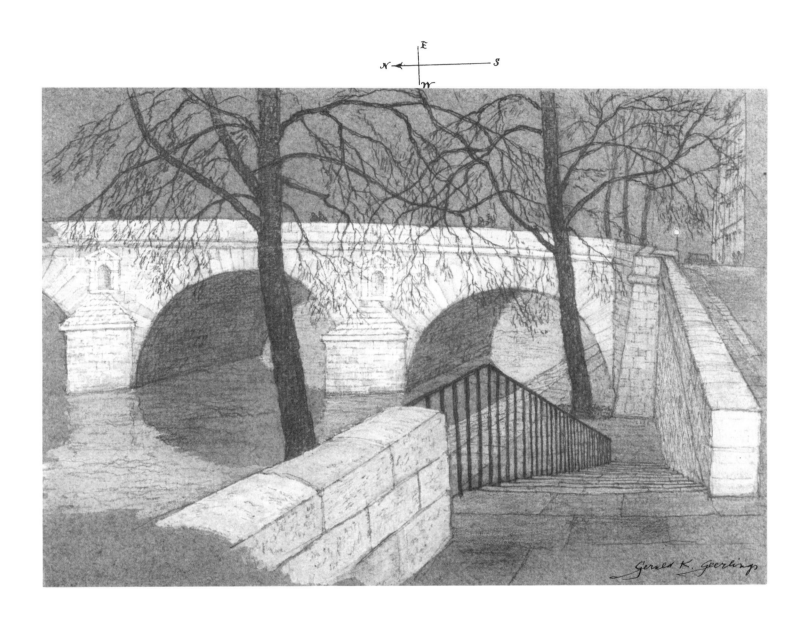

The Pont Marie viewed from the Quai de Bourbon on the Ile Saint-Louis

Île St. Louis in distance beyond Seine   Right Bank in foreground

1-Rue Fauconnier   A-Quai d'Anjou   B-Quai des Célestins   2-Rue du Figuier

A view of the Ile Saint-Louis across the Bibliothèque Forney on the Right Bank

1-Rue des Barres /2-Rue Grenier-sur-l'Eau /3-Right Bank end of Pont Louis-Philippe /4-Quai de Bourbon (Île St. Louis)

5-Garden at apse of St. Gervais

Looking south from the Church Saint-Gervais, rue des Barres

Île St. Louis   Île de la Cité   Right Bank

B - Quai aux Fleurs   1 - Pont d'Arcole with Pont Nôtre Dame beyond

A - Quai de Bourbon   C - Quai de Hotel de Ville

The Pont Louis-Philippe as viewed from the Quai de Bourbon

Île St. Louis | Left Bank | Île de la Cité

Gerrey K. Geerlings

A - Quai de Hotel de Ville   1 - Panthéon   2 - Nôtre Dame   B - Quai aux Fleurs

View from the Right Bank end of the Pont Louis-Philippe, looking south and southwest toward the Panthéon and Notre-Dame

Île de la Cité   Right Bank

1-Hôtel Dieu   2-Pont d'Arcole   3-Pedestrian bridge over Autoroute des Berges

A-Quai aux Fleurs   B-Quai de Hôtel de Ville

A small park between the Pont Louis-Philippe and the Pont d'Arcole

A- Quai de Hotel de Ville / 1-Pont Louis-Philippe / C- West end of Ile St. Louis and Quai de Bourbon / D- Quai de la Tournelle   E- Quai aux Fleurs
B -Little park with pedestrian bridge over vehicular traffic   2- Pont St. Louis

The Pont Louis-Philippe and the Pont Saint-Louis viewed from a small park on the Right Bank

S

W   E

N

Île St. Louis   Left Bank (background)

East end of Île de la Cité (foreground)

A-Quai de Bourbon (aboré)   1-Pont St. Louis   2-Pantheon   B-Quai aux Fleurs

The Pont Saint-Louis viewed from the west end of the Ile Saint-Louis

1-Two Theatres (Châtelet and de la Ville) on Place du Châtelet / 2-Tour St. Jacques / 3-Hôtel de Ville / 4-Pont Nôtre Dame
A-Quai aux Fleurs　　　　B-Lower quai at west end of Île St. Louis　　　　C-Quai de Hôtel de Ville

The Pont d'Arcole viewed from the west end of the Ile Saint-Louis

A-Quai de Gesvres   1-Tour St. Jacques   2-Hotel de Ville   B-Quai de Hotel de Ville

The Pont d'Arcole viewed from the Ile de la Cité

1-Hôtel Dieu / 2-Spire of Ste. Chapelle / 3-Dome of Tribune de Commerce / 4-Four Towers of Conciergerie
A-Quai de la Corse / 5-Louvre / 6-Theatre du Châtelet / 7-Pont au Change with Pont Neuf beyond / B-Quai de Gesvres

The Pont Notre-Dame viewed from the Pont d'Arcole

1-Tribunal de Commerce/2-Tour de l'Horloge and Conciergerie/3-Louvre/4-Pont Neuf/5-Pont au Change/6-Pont Notre Dame
A-Quai de la Corse

The Ile de la Cité as viewed from the Pont Notre-Dame looking west

A - Quai de la Corse   1 - Theatre de la Ville   2 - Tour St. Jacques   B - Quai de Gesvres

Flower Market on the Ile de la Cité, Place Louis-Lépine

Right Bank

A - Quai de Gesvres   1 - Place du Châtelet   2 - Théâtre de la Ville   3 - Tour St. Jacques

The Pont Notre-Dame viewed from the Ile de la Cité looking toward the Right Bank

90

Ile de Ja Cité

1-Hôtel Dieu   2-Spire of Nôtre Dame   3-Twin Towers of Nôtre Dame   4-Tribune de Commerce

A-Quai de Ja Megisserie   5-Tour de l'Horloge (Conciegerie)   6-Spire of Ste. Chapelle   B-Quai de l'Horloge

The Pont-au-Change looking toward the Ile de la Cité from the Right Bank

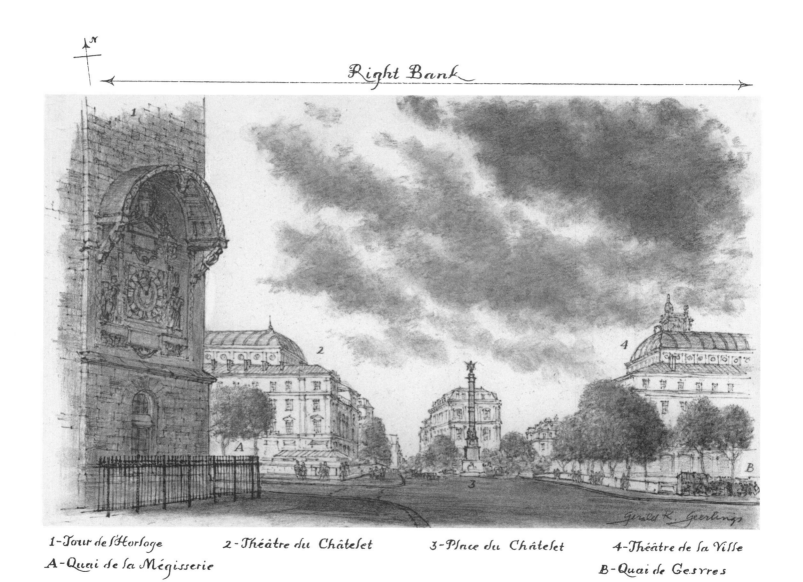

1-Tour de l'Horloge   2-Théâtre du Châtelet   3-Place du Châtelet   4-Théâtre de la Ville
A-Quai de la Mégisserie   B-Quai de Gesvres

View from the Tour de l'Horloge on the Ile de la Cité, looking across the Pont-au-Change

1-Theatre du Châtelet   2-Tour St. Jacques   3-Theatre de la Ville   4-Hôtel de la Ville   5-Tour de César (Conciergerie)

A-Quai de la Mégisserie   6-Pont au Change   B-Quai de l'Horloge

The Pont-au-Change and the Right Bank as viewed from the Conciergerie

Île de la Cité

The Conciergerie viewed from the Right Bank

1 – Place du Châtelet with two theatres / 2 – Hôtel de Ville / 3 – Hôtel Dieu / 4 – Conciergerie (north part of Palais de Justice)

A – Quai de la Mégisserie   and St. Gervais   B – Quai de l'Horloge

The Pont-au-Change viewed from the Pont-Neuf

A - Quai de l'Horloge   1 - Dome of Institut   2 - Tour Eiffel   B - Quai de la Mégisserie

The Pont-Neuf viewed from the Right Bank looking downstream

1-Pont au Change   2-Pont Nôtre Dame   3-Hotel de Ville

Under the Pont-Neuf on the Ile de la Cité looking upstream

Left Bank   N   Right Bank

A-Quai de Conti / 1-Palais du Louvre, Pavillon de Flore / 2-Place du Neuf behind statue of Henry IV / B-Quai du Louvre

The Square du Vert-Galant as viewed from the Pont-Neuf

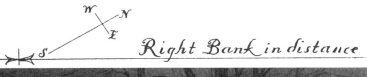

Left Bank in distance   Right Bank in distance

Statue of Henri **IV** and to right: Arc de Triomphe and Louvre

The Arc de Triomphe as viewed from the Place Dauphine

Île de la Cité   Left Bank in distance

N

Houses on Place Dauphine   Statue of Henri IV

The Right Bank arm of the Pont-Neuf, viewed from the Right Bank

100

A-Quai du Louvre /1-Hôtel de Ville /2-Conciergerie. /3-Spire of Ste. Chapelle /4-Place du Pont Neuf /5-Pantheon /B-Quai de Conti

The Pont-Neuf viewed from the Right Bank

A–Quai de Conti / 1–Pont du Carrousel with Pont Royal beyond / 2–Pavillon de Flore (west end of Louvre) / 3–East end of Louvre / B – Quai du Louvre

The Pont des Arts viewed from the west end of the Ile de la Cité

Île de la Cité   Left Bank   N

1-Pont Neuf   2-Square du Vert Galant   3-Hotel des Monnaies   4-Palais de l'Institut   5-Pont des Arts

A-Quai de Conti   B-Quai du Louvre

The Quai de Conti viewed from the Quai du Louvre across the Seine

1-Pont des Arts

A-Quai Malaquais

The Institut de France viewed from the Quai du Louvre on the Right Bank

Right Bank   Île de la Cité   Left Bank

A - Quai du Louvre   1 - Place du Châtelet with two theatres   2 - Pont Neuf   B - Place de l'Institut   C - Quai Malaquais

The Pont des Arts viewed from the Quai Malaquais

View from lower level, looking toward upper level of Quai Malaquais

View from upper level of Quai Malaquais, looking across Seine toward Louvre

Trees on the Quai Malaquais

Illuminated against sky from left to right: Spire of Ste. Chapelle, Nôtre Dame, Palais de l'Institut

View through the arch of the Pont du Carrousel on the Right Bank looking upstream

A-Quai des Tuileries / 1-Cour au Carrousel / 2-Louvre / B-Quai du Louvre / C-Quai Voltaire

The Pont du Carrousel from the Quai Voltaire on the Left Bank

A-Quai des Tuileries   1-Dome, Palais de l'Institute   B-Quai Voltaire

The Pont du Carrousel from the Quai du Louvre looking upstream

A-Quai des Tuileries   B-Quai du Louvre   1-Louvre   2-Pont des Arts with Pont Neuf beyond   C-Quai Voltaire

The Pont du Carrousel viewed from the Left Bank

W
S ——→ N
E

Left Bank   Right Bank

above bridge: Gare d'Orsay   above: Quai des Tuileries

The Pont-Royal viewed from the Right Bank end of the Pont du Carrousel

A-Quai Voltaire 1- Gare d'Orsay 2-Piscine Royal B-Quai des Tuileries

The Pont-Royal looking downstream to the Left Bank

Left Bank | Right Bank

1-Pont Solférino with Pont de la Concorde beyond   2-Grand Palais

A-Quai Voltaire   B-Quai des Tuileries

Looking downstream under the arches of the Pont-Royal on the Left Bank

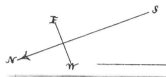

1-Arc de Triomphe du Carrousel   2-Pavillon de Flore   A-Quai des Tuileries

The Musée du Louvre from the Jardin des Tuileries

Right Bank

1-Arc de Triomphe   2-Pavillon de Flore   A-Quai Anatole France

The Musée du Louvre as viewed from the Place du Carrousel looking south

N

A-Rue de Rivoli   1-Statue of Jeanne d'Arc   2-Pavillon de Marsan

The Place des Pyramides from the Place du Carrousel looking north

116

A-Quai des Tuileries / 1-Jardin des Tuileries / 2-Rue de Rivoli / 3-Pavillon de Flore at west end of Louvre / B-Quai du Louvre / C-Quai Anatole France

The Pont-Royal and the Pavillon de Flore viewed from across the Seine on the Left Bank

Left Bank

A

N

A-Quai Anatole France

B – Quai des Tuileries

The pool Pont-Royal from the Quai des Tuileries (has been destroyed)

Right Bank ⟶ Left Bank N

A-Quai des Tuileries   1-Pavillon de Flore   2-Underground Autoroute   3-Pont Royal   B-Quai Anatole France

The Pont-Royal viewed from the Jardin des Tuileries

N

Left Bank ✕ Right Bank

A-Quai Anatole France   1-Pont Solférino   2-Jardin des Tuileries   B-Quai des Tuileries

The upper level pedestrian walk along the express way along the Jardin des Tuileries

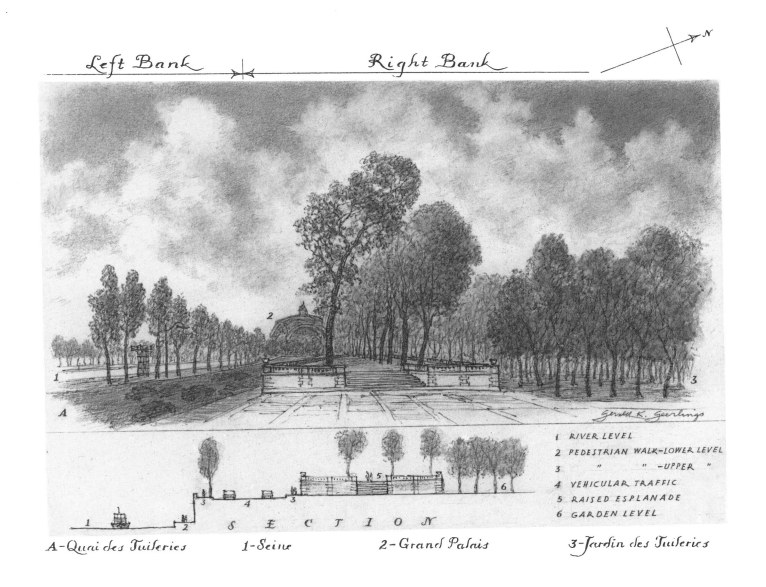

Left Bank | Right Bank | N

A — Quai des Tuileries   1 — Seine   2 — Grand Palais   3 — Jardin des Tuileries

1 RIVER LEVEL
2 PEDESTRIAN WALK–LOWER LEVEL
3   "   " –UPPER "
4 VEHICULAR TRAFFIC
5 RAISED ESPLANADE
6 GARDEN LEVEL

SECTION

Gerald K. Geerlings

View from the esplanade of the Tuileries garden looking west

Right Bank   Île de la Cité   Left Bank

1-Pavillon de Flore (Louvre) / 2-Hôtel de Ville / 3- Spire of Ste. Chapelle / 4-Nôtre Dame / 5-Palais de l'Institut / 6- Gare d'Orsay

The Pont-Royal viewed from the Pont Solferino looking upstream

A - Quai des Tuileries   1 - Jardin des Tuileries   2 - Masonry of bridge demolished in 1961   B - Quai Anatole France

The Pont Solferino viewed from the Left Bank looking north to the Jardin des Tuileries

Right Bank | Left Bank | N↗

A-Quai des Tuileries 1-Pont Royal 2-Gare d'Orsay (1900) 3-Palais de la Légion d'Honneur (1792) B-Quai Anatole France

The Pont Solferino viewed from the Right Bank looking upstream

A- Quai des Tuileries   1-Pavillon de Flore (west end of Louvre)   2-Pont Royal   3- Gare d'Orsay   B- Quai Anatole France

The Pont Solferino viewed from the Left Bank looking upstream

1-Assemblée Nationale   2-Ministére des Affairs Étrangères   3-Grand Palais   4-Petit Palais   5-Place de la Concorde   6-Ohélisque de Louqsor

A - Quai Anatole France   B - Quai des Tuileries

The Pont de la Concorde viewed from the Left Bank looking downstream

Right Bank

A-Quai de la Conference 1-U.S.Embassy 2-Obélisque de Louqsor 3-Sacre-Coeur 4-Opera B-Quai d'Orsay

The Pont de la Concorde and the Place de la Concorde as viewed from the Left Bank

E
S
N
W

Right Bank · Île de la Cité · Left Bank

A-Quai de la Conférence / 1-Louvre / 2-Ste. Chapelle / 3-Nòtre Dame / 4-Gare d'Orsay / 5-Assemblée National / B-Quai d'Orsay

The Pont de la Concorde viewed from the Cours la Reine on the Right Bank looking upstream

1-Obélisque de Louqsor   2-Ministère de la Marine   3-Jardin des Tuileries

The Place de la Concorde as viewed from the Orangerie in the Tuileries garden

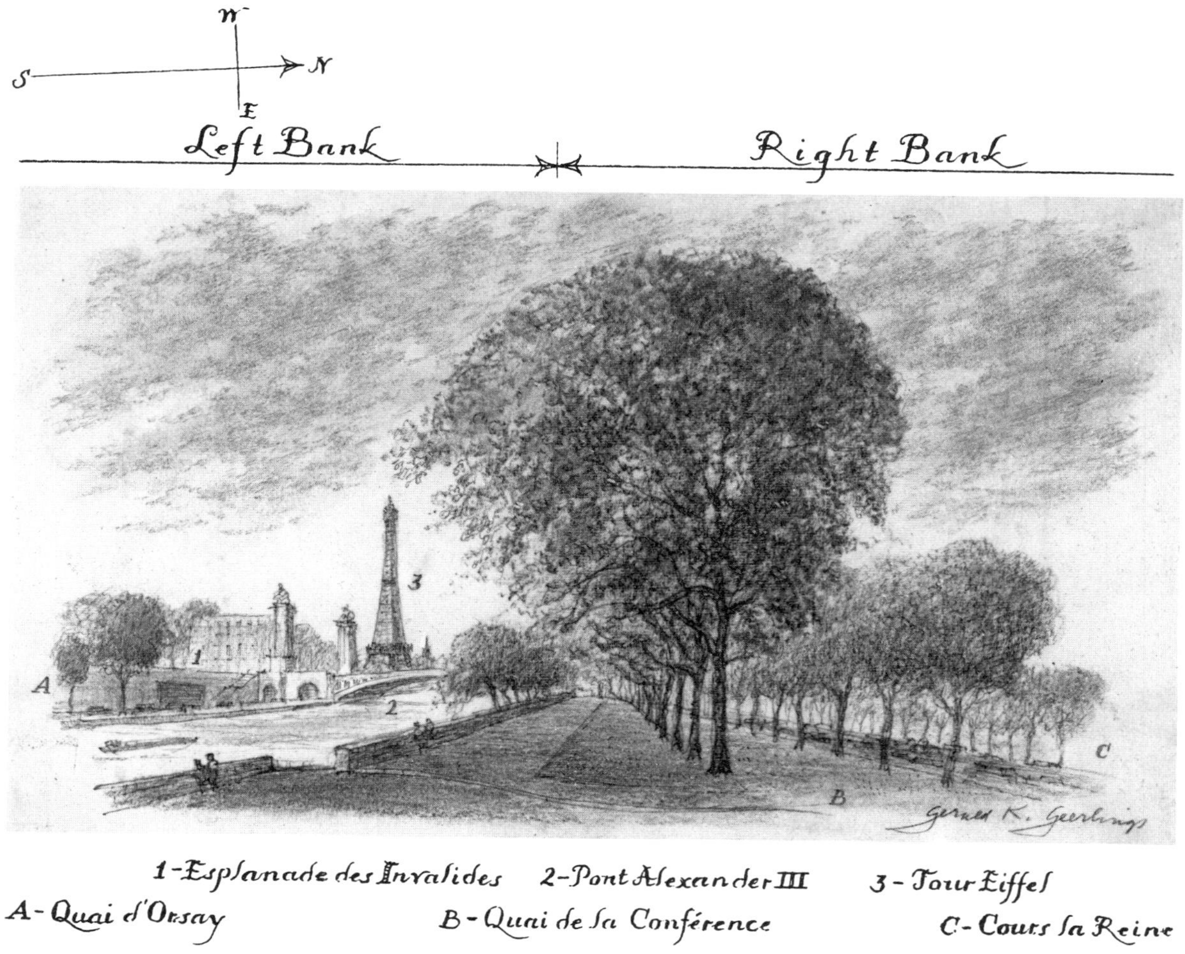
W
S
N
E
Left Bank
Right Bank
A
1
2
3
B
C
1-Esplanade des Invalides
2-Pont Alexander III
3-Tour Eiffel
A-Quai d'Orsay
B-Quai de la Conférence
C-Cours la Reine

The Eiffel Tower viewed from the Cours la Reine looking downstream

A-Quai d'Orsay   1-Tour Eiffel   2-American Church   3-Pont des Invalides   B-Quai de la Conference

The Pont Alexandre III viewed from the Port des Champs-Elysées looking downstream

Left Bank

Frontal view of the Hôtel des Invalides viewed from the Right Bank side of the Pont Alexandre III

The Cour d'Honneur of the Hôtel des Invalides looking north toward the Seine

The Dôme des Invalides viewed from the Cour d'Honneur

A-Quai d'Orsay   1-Grand Palais   2-Petit Palais   B-Quai de la Conférence

The Pont Alexandre III as seen from the Left Bank across the Grand Palais

The sunken garden adjacent to the Seine at the S-W corner of the Grand Palais

A- Quai d'Orsay   1-American Church   2- Tour Eiffel   B- Quai de la Conférence

The Pont des Invalides viewed from the Right Bank looking downstream

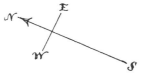

A-Quai de la Conférence   1-Grand Palais   2-Pylons of Pont Alexander III   B-Quai d'Orsay

The Pont des Invalides viewed from the Left Bank looking upstream

N ← | → S   Right Bank | Left Bank

A - Quai de la Conférence / 1 - Grand Palais / 2 - American Church / B - Quai d'Orsay

The esplanade along the Quai d'Orsay looking upstream

A - Quai d'Orsay   1 - Tour Eiffel   2 - Palais de Chaillot   B - Quai de la Conférence

The Pont de l'Alma and the Eiffel Tower viewed from the Right Bank looking downstream

The statue of the Zouave at the Right Bank end of the Pont de l'Alma as viewed from the Left Bank

Left Bank   *Right Bank*   N

A-Quai d'Orsay   *1-Passerelle Debilly in distance*   *2-Musée d'Art Moderne*   *B-Quai de la Conférence*

The Pont de l'Alma as viewed from the Left Bank looking downstream

Left Bank   Right Bank

A - Quai Branly   B - Avenue de New York

The Passerelle Debilly viewed from the Right Bank looking downstream

N
W — E
S

A - Avenue de New York   1 - Musée d'Art Moderne   B - Quai Branly

The Passerelle Debilly viewed from the Quai Branly looking north

143

The Musée d'Art Moderne on the Avenue de New York on the Right Bank

Left Bank in distance beyond Seine

A view of the Seine from under the colonnades of the Musée d'Art Moderne

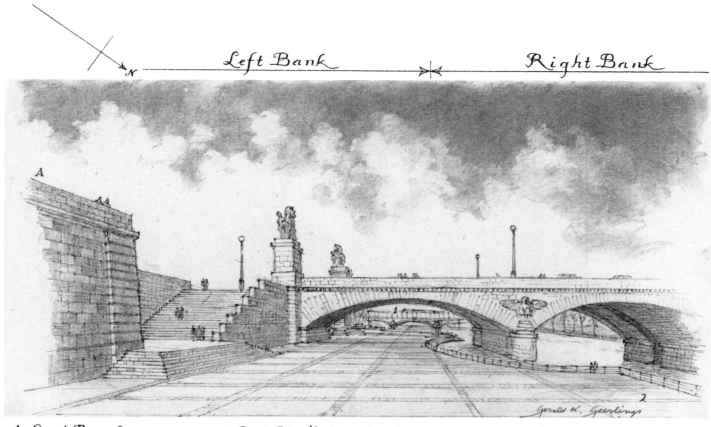

Left Bank | Right Bank

A-Quai Branly   1-Pont Bir-Hakeim in distance   2-Port de la Bourdonnais

Looking downstream from under the Left Bank end of the Pont d'Iéna

A and B-Avenue de New York   1-Palais de Chaillot   2-Parc du Trocadéro   C- Quai Branly

The Pont d'Iéna viewed from the Left Bank across to the Palais de Chaillot

The Palais de Chaillot viewed from the west side esplanade

Left Bank

S
E
N
W

1-Sainte-Clotilde　　2-Saint-Sulpice　　3-Panthéon　　4-Hôtel des Invalides

Panoramic view of the Left Bank as seen from the Palais de Chaillot

A pond under the Eiffel Tower

N

A-Avenue du President Kennedy   1-Palais de Chaillot   2-Parc du Trocadéro   3-Tour Eiffel

Quai Branly looking upstream at the Right Bank

A–*Avenue de New York*   1–*Tour Eiffel*   B–*Quai Branly*

The Pont d'Iéna viewed from the Right Bank looking upstream

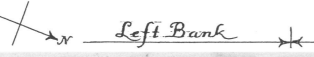

A-Quai Branly   1-Île de Cygnes (east end)   B-Avenue de New York

The Pont Bir-Hakeim viewed from the Quai Branly looking downstream

153

View of the Right Bank part of the Pont Bir-Hakeim as seen from the Allée des Cygnes

A-Allée des Cygnes /1-Railroad Bridge /2-Office de Radiodiffussion Television Française (O.R.T.F.) /B-Avenue du Pres. Kennedy

The Right Bank of the Railroad Bridge as viewed from the Allée des Cygnes looking downstream

155

A-Quai Louis Blériot   1-Office de Radiodiffussion Télévision Française (O.R.T.F.)   B-Port St. Javel
2-Île des Cygnes

The Pont de Grenelle and the west tip of the Allée des Cygnes with the original Statue of Liberty as viewed from the Left Bank

1-Pont de Grenelle / 2-Pedestrian walkway / 3-Office de Radiodiffussion Television Française (O.R.T.F.)
A-Avenue du Pres. Kennedy / 4-Allée des Cygnes / 5-Tour Eiffel / 6-Railroad bridge / B-Quai de Grenelle

The Maison de la Radio as viewed from under the pedestrian walkway of the Pont de Grenelle looking N-E

A - Quai André Citröen   1 - Pont Mirabeau   B - Quai Louis Blériot

The Pont Mirabeau as viewed from the Pont de Grenelle looking downstream

Paris Along The Seine

Typographical Composition in Goudy Old Style Regular and Italic by Typo Arts, Stamats Communications, Inc., Cedar Rapids, Iowa.

Offset Lithography, on Superfine Mohawk 60 lb. text and 15 lb. Roncote Cambric Cover by Stamats Communications, Inc., Cedar Rapids, Iowa.

Binding by W. A. Krueger.

Book Design by Stamats Communications, Inc.

6,000 copies (1,000 cloth) of this book have been published by the Cedar Rapids Museum of Art and the French Institute/Alliance Francaise in 1987.

50 copies of this book have been issued as a limited edition with an original signed sepia lithograph, *Paris — Toward the Louvre from the Pont Saint-Michel* (1986) by Gerald K. Geerlings. The lithograph was printed by Steven B. Miller of George C. Miller & Son, Inc., New York.

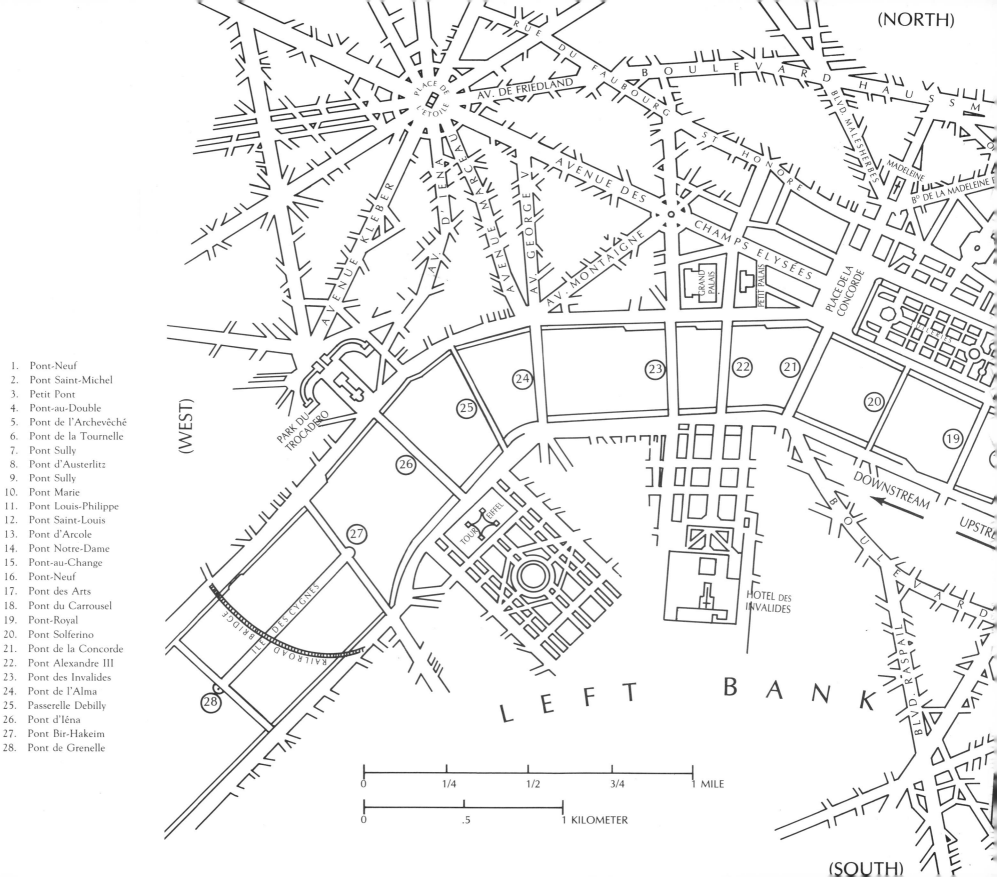

(NORTH)

1. Pont-Neuf
2. Pont Saint-Michel
3. Petit Pont
4. Pont-au-Double
5. Pont de l'Archevêché
6. Pont de la Tournelle
7. Pont Sully
8. Pont d'Austerlitz
9. Pont Sully
10. Pont Marie
11. Pont Louis-Philippe
12. Pont Saint-Louis
13. Pont d'Arcole
14. Pont Notre-Dame
15. Pont-au-Change
16. Pont-Neuf
17. Pont des Arts
18. Pont du Carrousel
19. Pont-Royal
20. Pont Solferino
21. Pont de la Concorde
22. Pont Alexandre III
23. Pont des Invalides
24. Pont de l'Alma
25. Passerelle Debilly
26. Pont d'Iéna
27. Pont Bir-Hakeim
28. Pont de Grenelle

(WEST)

LEFT BANK

(SOUTH)